THE ARCHAEOLOGY OF THE WELS

The solitary hillfort of Dinas, near Ponterwyd in Ceredigion, looks down on a landscape
of bare hills and deep valleys in the foothills of the Plynlimon mountain range. 2001-cs-1924

(opposite) Ynysypandy, Gwynedd. The large three-storey mill built to fabricate products bought down from
the nearby Gorseddau slate quarries. A large water wheel inside the building provided power, with slate delivered
from a tramway entering the mill by the curving siding. The small waste tips close by attest to how little material
was actually processed. The mill is in the ownership of the Snowdonia National Park Authority. 93-cs-1097

THE ARCHAEOLOGY OF THE WELSH UPLANDS

Edited by
David Browne & Stephen Hughes

ROYAL COMMISSION ON THE ANCIENT AND HISTORICAL MONUMENTS OF WALES

Sponsored by Welsh Assembly Government

Royal Commission on the Ancient and Historical Monuments of Wales

Plas Crug, Aberystwyth, Ceredigion, SY23 1NJ

Telephone: 01970 621200   *Fax:* 01970 627701
e-mail: nmr.wales@rcahmw.org.uk   *Web page:* www.rcahmw.org.uk

Printed in Wales by: Cambrian Printers Limited
Llanbadarn Road, Aberystwyth, Ceredigion, SY23 3TN.   *Telephone:* 01970 613027

EDITORIAL NOTE AND ACKNOWLEDGEMENTS

Stephen Hughes and David Browne have been responsible for the content and copy editing respectively of this book, with help from the editorial committee team of Robert Silvester of the Clwyd-Powys Archaeological Trust and Toby Driver and David Leighton of RCAHMW. The members of the Uplands Initiative Steering Committee under the chairmanship of Professor Geoffrey Wainwright have overseen the evolution of the book. The aerial photographs were taken by Toby Driver and Chris Musson. Photographs on pages 83 (bottom) and 108 were taken by Nigel Jones of CPAT as regional flyer for RCAHMW. Particular thanks are due to the following: Professor David Austin and the Department of Archaeology students from the University of Wales, Lampeter, who helped survey the hushing leats at Cwmystwyth Mine; Susan Jones and Andrew Dutton for their work on the Moel Bronymiod and Bwlch Mawr surveys; the Commandant and staff at the Sennybridge Training Area, particularly Jonathan Jackson, who did so much to assist archaeologists with access to sites on the range and also drew attention to additional monuments. The Epynt air-photo mapping project could not have progressed smoothly without the help of the Secretary and staff of the Royal Commission, particularly Chris Musson, Terry James and Nick Glanville; the success of the project owed much to considerable groundwork by Dr Stephen Briggs. The ground survey on Epynt formed part of the Cadw-funded Deserted Rural Settlements programme, and thanks are due to Cadw, and particularly Dr Mike Yates and Dr Kate Roberts, for permission to incorporate some of the results of that programme in the article in this book.

The source of each illustration is given after its caption. Unless otherwise stated, the reference numbers relate to the National Monuments Record of Wales's collection, and the latter should be quoted in any application for copies from the Royal Commission.

CONTENTS

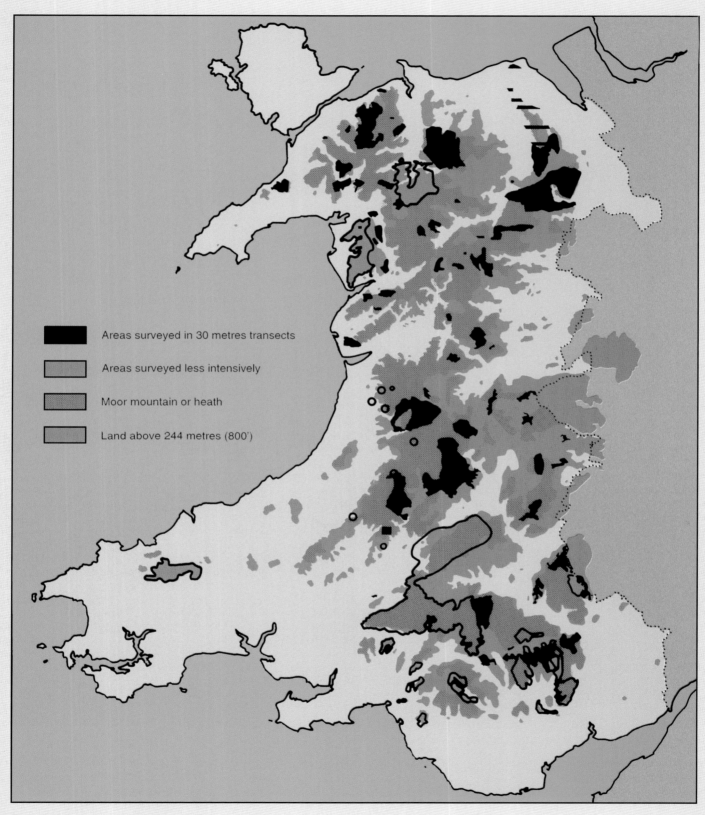

Areas surveyed in 30 metres transects

Areas surveyed less intensively

Moor mountain or heath

Land above 244 metres (800')

FOREWORD

Gone are the days when archaeologists were content to describe ruins and objects to a small group of like-minded enthusiasts. The fate of a Tudor theatre in London or a medieval boat in Newport can catch the national imagination and inspire public demonstrations in favour of their protection and retention. It is now generally recognised that archaeology forms part of an interlocking mosaic of elements which make up our cultural heritage and which include archaeological sites and historic buildings a s well as hedgerows, natural landscapes, public parks, local history and language that comprise our understanding of the past and who we are. Archaeology is about learning from the past and using that understanding as a catalyst for economic and social change. That awareness combines with other elements of the historic environment to improve the quality of our lives through an enhanced sense of place and our sense of citizenship. It can generate prosperity, regenerate our towns and countryside and through public access and involvement lead to a deeper sense of community. Public enthusiasm for our heritage is strong - the intensive prime-time media focus on archaeology and history reaches an audience of millions - and the custodians of the remains of our past are made well aware - repeatedly and emphatically - that they will be held to public account for the quality of their care.

Wales is fortunate in that our historic environment is a rich national resource which includes the remains of our stone age ancestors from caves in north and south Wales, the source of the building materials for Stonehenge in the Preseli Hills of north Pembrokeshire, stone circles, Roman forts, Celtic crosses, medieval castles, the remains of the Industrial Revolution and structures from the Second World War. These archaeological remains are a massive draw for tourists and a major contribution to the economy of rural Wales as well as our cities. Many more sites remain to be discovered and our understanding of them deepened and strengthened. The Royal Commission on the Ancient and Historical Monuments of Wales exists for the purpose of undertaking such high-quality surveys and investigations as an essential prerequisite for policy making by government, local authorities, Cadw, National Parks and the Countryside Council for Wales, and to ensure that national and regional records are both comprehensive and accessible to schools, the public and academics through the use of electronic media.

The archaeological remains of the upland areas of Wales are extensive, well-preserved and largely unrecorded. They were therefore a prime target for a survey project by the Royal Commission. It is possible to walk across great tracts of Welsh upland, from Strumble Head to Foel Drygarn in north Pembrokeshire or from Snowdon to the Lleyn with the realisation that one is not only walking through some of the most beautiful countryside in the United Kingdom but also through relic landscapes largely unchanged in some areas for the past 4000 years. The cairns, field walls, standing stones, enclosures and hillforts can actually be touched and walked upon and seen in relation to each other and therefore have a great deal to offer in terms of creating and enhancing a vivid understanding of our past. The survey of the remains also enables the development of preservation strategies to protect them for the future, provides an essential education resource with the right access to the information, and the new information gained will contribute to economic regeneration through managed tourism and conservation grant schemes such as *Tir Gofal*.

The results of the first ten years of the Uplands Initiative have been summarised in this book, which has been written for the general public as well as the archaeologist because it deals with a subject that is vital to the quality of all our lives- not just to the few - and to the sense of ourselves as a nation.

Geoffrey Wainwright
Former Vice-chairman RCAHMW & Chair of the Uplands Steering Committee.

(opposite) The progress of the Uplands Initiative.
Map of the uplands of Wales defined by the 800-feet (244-metre) contour, showing open land and those areas already surveyed.

(overleaf) Names of the main blocks of the uplands of Wales mentioned in the text.

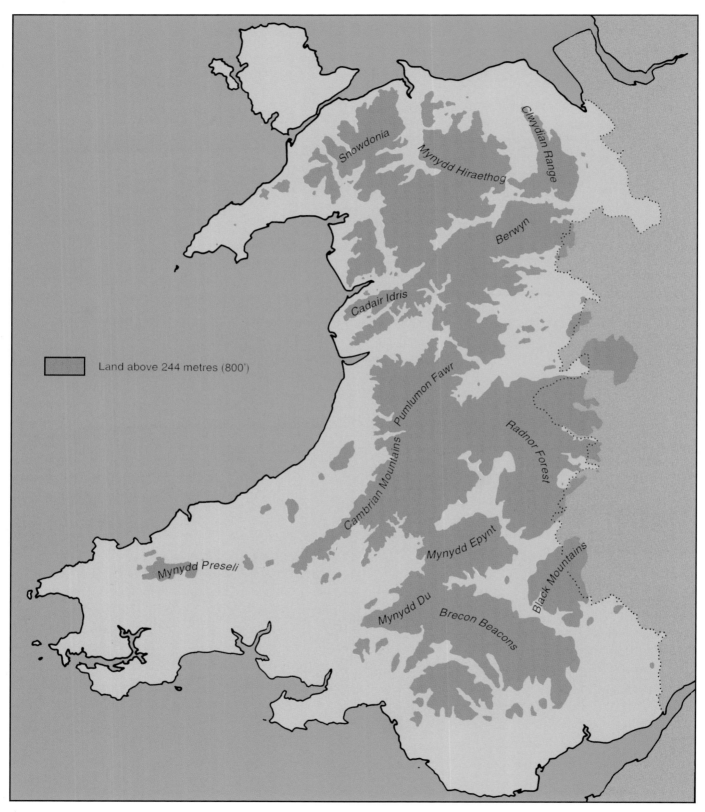

Land above 244 metres (800')

Snowdonia

Mynydd Hiraethog

Clwydian Range

Berwyn

Cadair Idris

Pumlumon Fawr

Cambrian Mountains

Radnor Forest

Mynydd Preseli

Mynydd Epynt

Black Mountains

Mynydd Du

Brecon Beacons

THE ARCHAEOLOGY OF THE WELSH UPLANDS:
AN INTRODUCTION

Robert Silvester (Clwyd-Powys Archaeological Trust)

Wales has always been characterised as a land of hills and mountains. From the comments of Giraldus Cambrensis in the twelfth century, through Daniel Defoe's sometimes caustic views in the early eighteenth century – 'even Hannibal himself would have found it impossible to have marched his army over Snowden [sic], or over the rocks of Merioneth and Montgomery shires'– to the later enthusiasms of The Romantics, the hills have been a focus for the traveller, as well as for the indigenous inhabitants. More than one third of Wales's 8,000 square miles lies above the 244-metres (800 feet) contour, which is generally accepted as the lower limit of the upland, and twenty-seven per cent lies above 304 metres (1000 feet), although this is not evenly distributed, with some regions, such as the south-west peninsula, the southern coastal strip and the island of Anglesey, having little true upland.

Some of the upland ranges are widely known: Snowdonia in Caernarfon, Cadair Idris in Meirionnydd, and the Cambrian Mountains, which form the mountainous spine down the centre of the country. Others are rather less well known. Llangollen is familiar to many for its festival, yet the Berwyn mountains towering over the town to the south and running for many miles down into Montgomeryshire are by comparison relatively unknown. Mynydd Preseli is famed for providing the raw material for the bluestones at Stonehenge, but the fact

Even the stark splendour of the highest peak in the Welsh uplands – Snowdon – is interrupted by manifestations of human endeavour. The present café just below the summit, with the railway terminal immediately behind it, is the modern successor to two inns that were there in the mid-nineteenth century. 94-cs-0979 (The National Library of Wales).

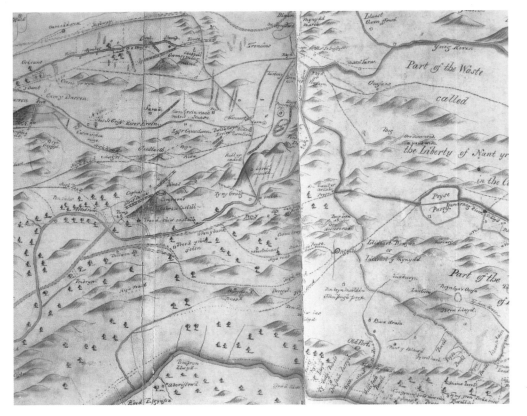

Lewis Morris's manuscript map of the 'mannor of Perveth', drawn in c.1745 and now in the National Library of Wales, displays a part of upland Ceredigion a century before most of the Welsh uplands was mapped for the first time. Rivers and roads provide a framework on the plan, while hills are shown schematically. The primary purpose of the commission from the Crown's Surveyor-General was to map the mines and metalliferous veins, but Morris also mapped hillforts and other prehistoric features. NLW RM A118 (The National Library of Wales).

that it is virtually the only block of hills in Pembrokeshire is less readily appreciated. The Welsh valleys are internationally known because of their past industry, but they would not exist without the high moorland ridges that separate them. The Brecon Beacons are renowned, but they form only the middle of a broad band of mountains and hills that run eastwards and westwards across the south part of the country; their eastward extension is the Black Mountains, their westward Fforest Fawr and the Black Mountain.

People have always used the hills, for as James Howell put it in 1621: 'our Mountains in Wales bear always something useful to Man or Beast' (Rees 1992, 44). They have provided the land for shelter and settlement; for burial and for the rituals that played such an important part at some periods in the past; for hunting, farming and other forms of subsistence; and for mining and industry. The nature of the landscape, its altitude and its remoteness have all influenced these activities to a greater or lesser degree. Generally, the more extreme one or more of these landscape characteristics become, the more restricted the range of activities that occurred. A remote mountainous area in Snowdonia, for instance, is unlikely to

have been utilised in the past in the same way as an upland common ringed by valleys in Radnorshire. Yet even on the highest points one cannot escape the impact of man: on Pen-y-fan and Corn-du, the remote summits of the Brecon Beacons, there are Bronze Age burial cairns; a railway winds its way to the summit of Snowdon, where a café is set; while on the crest of Cadair Idris a shelter has been built for walkers. It is how past generations have lived, worked and died in the hills, and the remains that they have left behind them, that is the concern of this volume.

History

The study of upland antiquities extends back for almost three hundred years. Learned clergymen and gentry of the eighteenth and nineteenth centuries recognised prehistoric 'tumuli' on the upland ridges for the burial mounds that they were and sometimes dug into them to carry away the 'rude earthen vessels' filled with the fragments of cremated bone of the Bronze Age dead. Interested surveyors began to depict on their maps upland features which we can now recognise only by archaeological means. Inveterate travellers like Thomas Pennant of Downside in Flintshire, who commented on the hillforts of the Clwydian range (Moore 1976, 203; Moore 1997), and Sir Richard Colt Hoare, a Wiltshire landowner and one of the great barrow diggers, whose interests took him throughout Wales (Thompson 1983), are amongst the most famous of a larger group whose records had an impact in the early days of archaeology. Iolo Morganwg (d.1826), a man of many parts - stonemason, poet and forger - has also been labelled 'Glamorgan's first field archaeologist' (Thomas 1984).

The mid-nineteenth century witnessed the establishment of the national Cambrian Archaeological Association and one or two regional societies (Silvester 1997b). Annual journals offered an outlet for the dissemination of ideas and discoveries, and it comes as no surprise to find as a commonplace descriptions of antiquities in the hills, as for instance when the Reverend C. Drinkwater illustrated early settlements in the hills around Bala in Meirionnydd (Drinkwater 1888), or when the clergy and gentlemen in Montgomeryshire enthusiastically set about writing the histories of their parishes for the newly established *Montgomeryshire Collections*. Furthermore, it was in the 1870s and 1880s that the Ordnance Survey conducted the first accurate large-scale survey of the Welsh uplands in preparation for the 6-inch 'County Series'.

With the formation of the Royal Commission on the Ancient and Historical Monuments and Constructions in Wales and Monmouthshire in 1908 archaeology entered the professional era. The Royal Commission prepared a series of

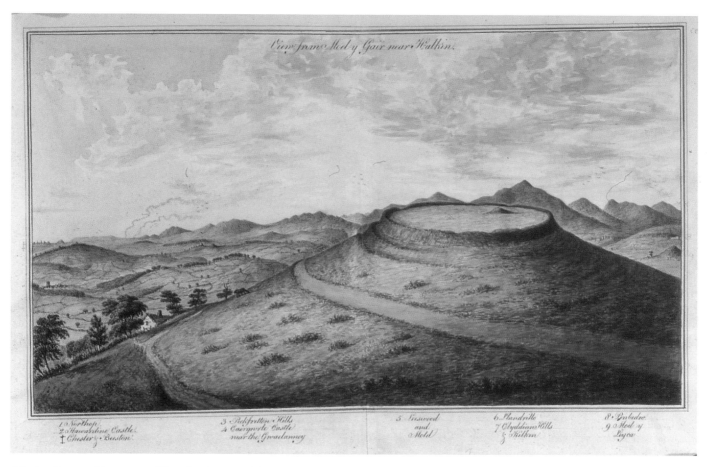

Moel y Gaer in Rhosesmor (Flintshire): one of the better known hillforts in north-east Wales, because of the important excavations there in the 1970s. Nearly two hundred years earlier it had been drawn by the artist John Ingleby, who depicted the Clwydian Hills in the background. While the drawing tells us nothing that cannot be established from fieldwork today, it does reflect the growing interest in upland antiquities in the second half of the eighteenth century. NLW/Prints/PD146 (The National Library of Wales).

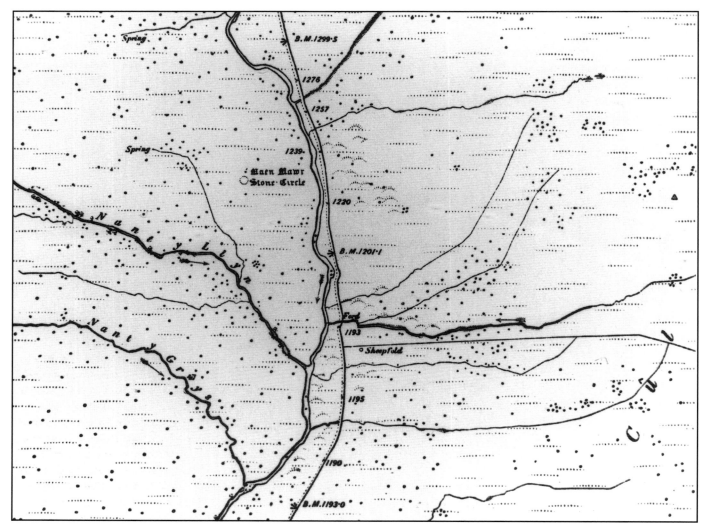

The Ordnance Survey mapped upland Brecknock in 1883-4, for the first time providing a detailed plan at a scale of 1:10560 of drainage patterns, roads and tracks. Historic landscape features were also shown, as here in the upper reaches of the River Tawe with not only sheepfolds but also the standing stone known as Maen Mawr and the stone circle immediately to the south of it. NLW Brecknock 38 NW

county volumes between 1911 (for Montgomeryshire) and 1925 (for Pembrokeshire), treating the man-made remains of both the uplands and lowlands. The Cambrian Archaeological Association encouraged the excavation of upland hillforts such as Tre'r Ceiri (Gwynedd) and Dinorben (Denbighshire) in the first two decades of the new century.

New standards of observation and field recording gradually developed, and archaeologists, professional and amateur, added further detail to the emerging picture. For north-east Wales Canon Ellis Davies produced two volumes on the prehistoric and Roman remains of Denbighshire (1929) and Flintshire (1949). Sir Cyril Fox of the National Museum of Wales in the early 1930s set out with his wife, Aileen, to research the moorlands of Glamorgan in preparation for a volume of the *Glamorgan County History*. During this work he puzzled over long platforms cut into the hillside of Gelligaer Common - on excavation these proved to be the bases for medieval houses, now recognised as one of the commonest types of earthwork in the uplands. Reconnaissance from the air, particularly by Dr J. K. S. St Joseph flying from

Cambridge in the 1950s through to the 1970s, did much to elucidate the pattern of Roman military activity in upland Wales, identifying for the first time large marching camps such as Plas-y-gors in the Brecon Beacons, which marked the movement of the Roman legions and their auxiliaries during the initial conquest of Wales during the first century AD. The Royal Commission's own staff in its assessments of Caernarfonshire, Glamorgan and Brecknock in the decades after the Second World War examined the extensive uplands of those counties, identifying large numbers of previously unrecognised signs of human activities, recording them in detail, and beginning to reveal just how much survived in the hills and, as importantly, how well preserved were the remains.

Throughout the 1970s and 1980s research continued in different parts of upland Wales, each programme undertaken in its own right, whether as fieldwork or excavation, rather than within the context of an overall policy for the uplands. In the early 1970s the imminent flooding of the remote Brenig Valley in the Denbigh Moors in north Wales provided Frances Lynch and her teams with an opportunity to investigate a cemetery of Bronze Age barrows and cairns, a *hafod* settlement and other upland sites (Lynch 1993). In the late 1970s the Torfaen Museum Trust surveyed the uplands around Blaenafon, its focus being the post-medieval and industrial remains. The establishment of the four Welsh Archaeological Trusts in 1974 gave a further impetus to upland work, not least in Gwynedd where surveys were undertaken in Ardudwy and Arthog (Kelly 1982; 1983). In the 1980s the National Archaeological Survey, part of the Royal Commission, examined a large tract of the Black Mountain and the western Brecon Beacons (Leighton 1997), while Anthony Ward worked on the Black Mountain in eastern Carmarthenshire (Ward 1988) and Peter Drewett undertook fieldwork on Mynydd Presceli in Pembrokeshire (Drewett 1987).

As a result of the various surveys conducted in the uplands some archaeologists began to appreciate that the hills and mountains concealed a vast quantity of remains in contrast to the much-ploughed lowlands, and allied to this they increasingly realised that sites and landscapes of all periods needed to be recorded, not just those of the prehistoric and Roman eras. Medieval and post-medieval remains were seen to be as significant for the story of the uplands as those of earlier days (see for instance Leighton 1997, 29).

Aerial photography has played a pivotal role in 'opening up' the uplands to study. Initially aerial reconnaissance was used for the identification of previously unrecognized sites.

Denbigh Moors/Hiraethog: a high view of the platform cairn Brenig 51 (SH 989 566), under excavation in 1974. Sealed beneath the cairn were traces of earlier, Beaker period occupation. The cairn itself was built in two stages. The first took the form of a broad, flat stone ring, 22 metres across and 7 metres wide, enclosing a central open area 8 metres in diameter. This open area, which probably had a ceremonial role, was ringed with twenty-six small standing stones. To one side was a single cremation burial of a child aged about eleven years old, whilst in the centre was a posthole that may originally have supported a totem pole. The central area was later haphazardly back-filled with stone and the whole finished off to form a flat, circular platform. Finds from Brenig 51 included two pottery urns, two flint knives and fragments of a bone pommel, which may once have formed the handle of a funerary knife. RCAHMW 710125

The value of employing air photographs to map archaeological sites in their landscapes emerged only fully in the 1980s, when the archaeology of the whole of Bodmin Moor in south-west England was mapped from the air as a preliminary to detailed field recording. Similar projects followed elsewhere, and in 1995 the process was adapted for Mynydd Epynt in southern Powys, the results of which are reported elsewhere in this book. Since that preliminary venture the Royal Commission has made considerable use of aerial mapping for other parts of upland Wales.

Moreover, knowledge of the changing environments in which people lived and worked in the past has grown, because a range of increasingly sophisticated scientific techniques has

Tomen y Mur: the Roman fort here, commanding a high, windy spot in the uplands of Snowdonia, is one the most complete Roman military complexes in Britain. The fort is a remarkable survival from the early Roman campaigns in north-west Wales, and this aerial view from the east shows a variety of features. The rectangular shape of the fort can be seen in the left background, surmounted by a circular, medieval castle-mound (motte). In the left foreground can be seen traces of the levelled Roman parade ground. In the right foreground, in a 'V' formed by a light-coloured minor road and a field wall, is the small oval military amphitheatre, which may have been built to compensate the soldiers for what was probably a difficult and remote posting. 96-cs-0507

been brought to bear on the study of soils, pollen, mollusca, plant remains and other palaeoenvironmental indicators. Some studies have been undertaken independently, others in conjunction with excavation programmes, but their overall potential can be assessed from two syntheses directed specifically at the Welsh landscape (Taylor 1980; Caseldine 1990), though an updated assessment is now overdue.

In 1932 Cyril Fox (Fox 1932) had drawn the distinction between what he termed the Lowland and Highland Zones of Britain, but it was not until the 1980s that the term 'uplands archaeology' became current, partly in response to wider concerns about changes in management practice in areas that had escaped intensive farming. Furthermore, it was at this time that systematic fieldwork to assess the nature and value of what is often called the 'archaeological resource' began to gain momentum.

The Uplands Initiative

In 1986 Timothy Darvill compiled a 'watershed' review for the Council for British Archaeology. Entitled *The Archaeology of the Uplands: a Rapid Assessment of Archaeological Knowledge and Practice*, Darvill's report detailed the historical importance of the uplands of both Wales and

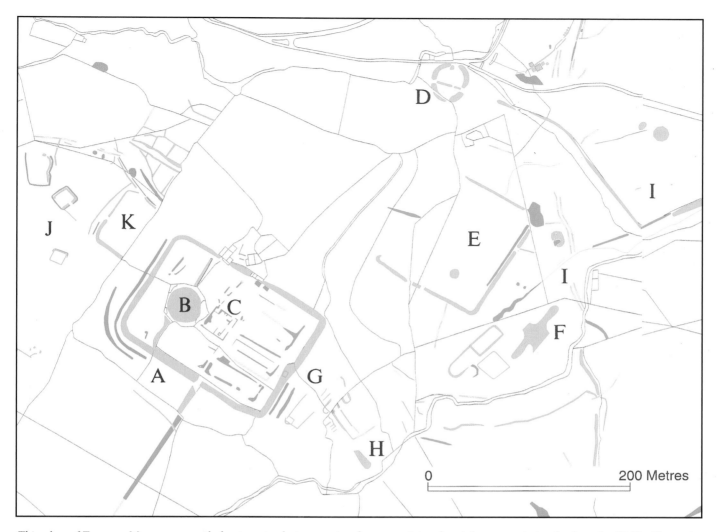

This plan of Tomen y Mur was compiled using air photo mapping from a variety of aerial sources dating back to the 1940s. The main fort can be seen (A) with the position of the medieval motte shown (B). Parchmarks photographed from the air in 1976 revealed the plan of the stone buildings inside the fort, including the headquarters building (C). The immediate environs of the fort preserve a fascinating array of monuments. Among these are the small military amphitheatre (D), and the levelled parade ground (E), which is overlooked by a tribunal mound (F). Outside the south-east gate of the fort the Roman road passes through the remains of a bathhouse and rest-house (G), a little obscured by the trenches of the nineteenth-century excavations. The road originally crossed the small river beyond via a wooden bridge, of which the 2.5 metres-high bridge abutment (H) still stands. Fragments of the water-supply system survive in the form of two leats (I) approaching from the north-east. On a hill to the north-west above the Roman fort are the remains of two or three small practice camps (J), together with the remains of an annex to the fort (K).

England, the variable state of knowledge about their many uses in the past, the threats to their archaeology, and the avenues that might be followed to ensure their survival (Darvill 1986a). In a shorter summary document – *Upland Archaeology: What Future for the Past?* – the opening section stated that 'the uplands constitute the largest single reserve of well-preserved historic landscape in Britain today' and that 'change is inevitable. But one of the marks of a civilised society is the care which it devotes to the management of change, so that our heritage is not unthinkingly disposed of, or

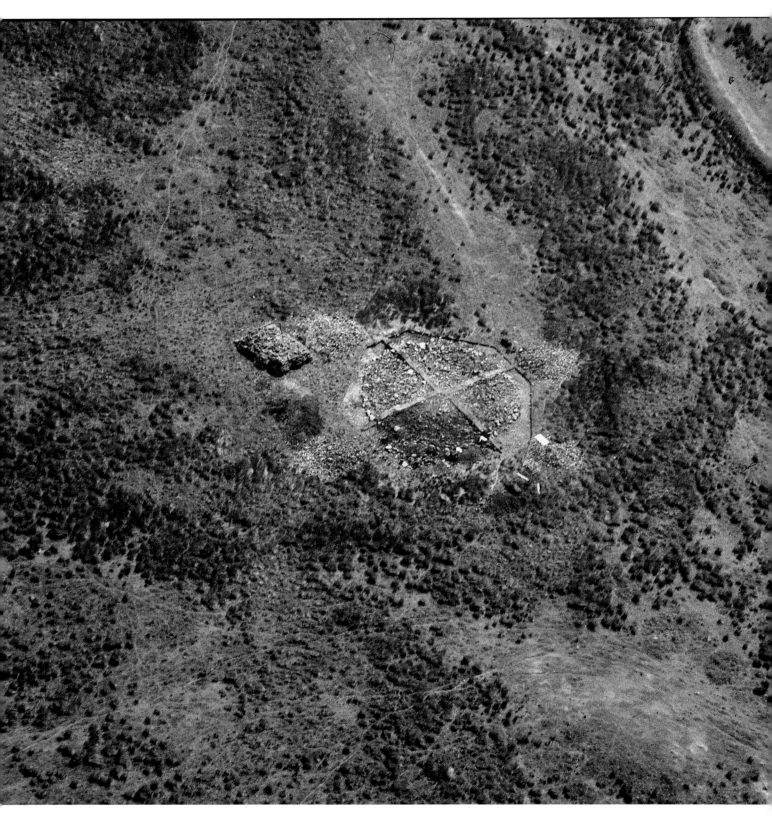

Two Bronze Age structured cairns were excavated at Carneddau in the uplands of western Montgomeryshire in 1989, revealing complex constructional sequences. 89-cs-798 Subsequently one of the cairns was reconstructed, leaving the low central mound grassed over and the kerbed ring of stone rubble exposed. The photo above was taken two years later, when the local community visited the site. CPAT Carneddau 163

squandered for short-term gain. Before such management can take place, there must be an awareness of what there is to be managed' (Darvill 1986b, 4).

Darvill's reports generated considerable interest and concern. Within a year Cadw: Welsh Historic Monuments had pioneered an 'Uplands Initiative' for Wales, commissioning the four Welsh Archaeological Trusts to assess the state of upland archaeology in their regions and to produce together a summary report of the then current situation (WAT n.d.).

1989 was a key year in the development of Welsh upland archaeology, when, for the first time, Cadw allocated resources specifically for the uplands, and systematic approaches were adopted to recording the archaeology of tracts of upland throughout the country. At Carneddau near Carno in northern Powys a group of prehistoric cairns was excavated and a post-medieval farmstead examined in advance of an afforestation scheme (Gibson 1993). Coupled with these excavations was a systematic field survey of some fifteen square kilometres of the surrounding hills (Silvester 1990), and elsewhere the Trusts embarked on a programme of detailed and methodical fieldwork targeted on selected uplands. Three years later the Royal Commission took over responsibility for running the Uplands Initiative and convened an annual gathering for those involved in uplands work, known as the Uplands Forum. Every year several projects were funded, typically extending across areas ranging from five to fifteen square kilometres and scattered throughout the Welsh uplands. Some surveys were recognised as trials to assess both the nature of the archaeology and its quality in a particular upland, while others evolved into longer programmes as the value of the initial work was appreciated. In the latter category was the four-year Mynydd y Ffynnon study (1996-99) of a block of land confined by the Rivers Wye, Rheidol and Ystwyth, spreading across the border zone of Powys and Ceredigion.

Some Trusts were also able to obtain funding from other bodies. Severn-Trent Water, for instance, sponsored a study of a medieval monastic grange known as the Llanwddyn Hospitium above Lake Vyrnwy (Silvester 1997c). Other assessments were completed as a result of development pressures on the uplands, notably in advance of the erection of upland windfarms. The Clwyd-Powys Archaeological Trust, for example, conducted a dozen windfarm surveys, ranging from small tracts of well under one square kilometre to much larger areas such as one on Mynydd Hiraethog in excess of thirteen square kilometres, which usefully complemented work previously completed in part of the same general area under the Uplands Initiative.

In 1999, after a decade of fieldwork, the Royal Commission decided to assess the achievements of the Initiative, which had by then engendered a substantial body of information. The timing was appropriate, because changes to the structuring of the fieldwork programme were emerging: organisations other than the Trusts, including the National Trust and the Denbighshire Archaeological Service, were bidding for funding for fieldwork and, following the satisfactory results from the Mynydd Epynt study, there was an increasing emphasis on the use of large-scale aerial mapping as a precursor to and guide during fieldwork programmes. Also, the Royal Commission was increasingly keen to determine which upland areas should be given priority, and to this end convened a permanent Uplands Steering Committee, representing organisations across Wales, to assess future strategy. In 1999-2000 each of the Trusts was commissioned to produce an overview of the uplands work conducted in their regions over the previous decade. One of the outcomes of that work is the present volume.

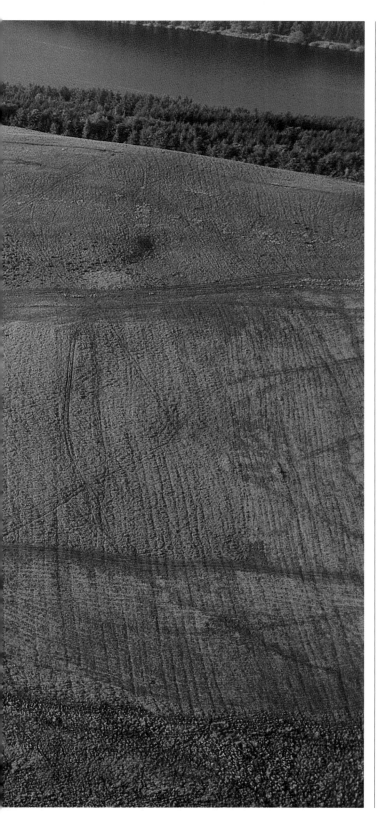

Purpose and practice

The archaeological content and potential of large areas of the uplands of Wales are still very poorly known. Field survey combined with aerial photographic mapping are the principal methods deployed to identify, record and understand the archaeology in the hills. Using these techniques we can build our knowledge and understanding of the many different ways in which earlier generations have utilised the uplands.

Under the Uplands Initiative various approaches have been adopted in the survey of particular uplands, some arguably more successful than others. Fieldwork techniques are now fairly standardised, with teams of archaeologists walking parallel transects across upland landscapes to identify all the archaeology. However, it is in the nature of the work that the sites and their landscape settings have to be examined and recorded quickly so that the surveys can be completed on time and within budget; usually there is no opportunity to linger at any particular site, even if it appears to be of signal interest, although it may be noted for detailed survey in the future, which may lead to it being designated as a 'site of national importance'. The main outcomes of survey are databases of sites, and a core index of this information is available on the CARN database accessible on line on the Royal Commission's web site. More than forty surveys have been completed, and the accompanying synthetic reports for each area are listed on the web site and can also be consulted in the National Monuments Record Library in Aberystwyth.

The collection of information has been the primary motivation of the surveys over the last decade; opportunities to study and analyse the data to achieve a coherent story have been few. The papers in this volume offer preliminary analyses of a few of the venues visited and of topics of interest identified during the Initiative. Also, several papers set the results of the Initiative to date in the context of previous research on the Welsh uplands.

The Llanwddyn Hospitium beneath a ridge on the south side of Lake Vyrnwy in northern Powys. The earthworks seen here are those of a grange (the centre of a farming estate) that was established about the beginning of the thirteenth century by the Knights Hospitallers religious order. The grange comprised a large rectangular building, terraced into the slope, with small embanked gardens or enclosures adjacent, a free-flowing spring still known as Ffynnon y Mynaich, and a ridged area that was used for cultivation - all within a larger enclosure. 99-cs-0318

Foel Cwm-Cerwyn, Mynydd Preseli, Pembrokeshire: a small cemetery of cairns along a ridge. One of the sites has produced an Early Bronze Age burial with an inverted urn. Many ridge-top cairns have survived because they have been incorporated into the unwritten definitions of medieval and later estate and parish boundaries. 99-cs-2309

THEMES & CHRONOLOGIES
THE UPLANDS DURING THE PREHISTORIC AND ROMAN PERIODS

Royal Commission on the Ancient and Historical Monuments of Wales

The Post-Glacial Environment

For most of the last million years much of Britain was covered by glacial ice. Long periods of ice advance were punctuated by shorter retreats, when the climate improved sufficiently for people to survive. There is excavated evidence from deposits laid down during one of these less severe phases *c.*230,000 years ago of the activities of Lower Palaeolithic (Old Stone Age) hunters in a cave at Pontnewydd in Clwyd (Green 1984). Later, Upper Palaeolithic hunters used the Gower caves during the last major interglacial about 25,000 years ago (Aldhouse-Green 2001; Green and Walker 1991). There is otherwise virtually no evidence for Palaeolithic people or their artefacts from most of inland or upland Wales (Aldhouse-Green 2000; Wymer 1999; Walker 2003).

After glaciers had retreated from Wales between *c.*14,000 and 10,000 BC, the climate slowly warmed. Following an initial periglacial episode, scrub vegetation, arctic shrubs and hardy woodland colonised the barren, boulder-strewn landscape (Campbell and Bowen 1989). It is very difficult to interpret the nature and extent of post-glacial settlement using only the known artefacts and excavated sites. However, people's relationship to their environment can be better appreciated from studying the pollen grains of the vegetation layers preserved in peat bogs (Caseldine 1990).

From their impact on the record of tree pollen, it appears that Mesolithic (Middle Stone Age) hunters and gatherers came into the early post-glacial environment in some numbers after *c.*7,500 BC (Aldhouse-Green 2000). Flint scatters, where broken or rejected blades are sometimes found mixed with waste flint flakes, demonstrate their presence occasionally over upland Wales (Barton *et al.* 1995). Among the many waste flints are diagnostic tool forms called microliths, which were cut to regular, geometric patterns; together with delicately-wrought arrowheads, they made up toolkits which included harpoons, scrapers and cutting tools (Green and Walker 1991).

Sometimes flint fragments weathering from beneath peat can hint at settlement sites where tents or other temporary structures were pitched. Occasionally, Mesolithic and later

Waun Fignen Felen, Brecknockshire: an upland peat bog formed on boulder clay deposited on limestone above a cave system. Investigation has shown it to have a pollen record which has provided considerable detail of climatic and vegetational change throughout the Post-Glacial Period. Evidence for Mesolithic settlement, in the form of microlithic chert industries, has been excavated in the area immediately surrounding the bog. 905511-12

flints have been found in upland (usually limestone) caves (RCAHMW 1997). Some caves and rock shelters are still accessible, and their lack of statutory protection from disturbance leaves them vulnerable to uncontrolled digging, which inevitably disturbs sediments which could be analysed for vital information about man's impact on the early environment.

The Neolithic

As an understanding of animal husbandry was developing in Britain during post-glacial times, ideas about plant husbandry were slowly spreading west from the Middle East. Destructive agricultural practices made steady inroads into European forests, until by *c.*4,000 BC they reached the British Isles.

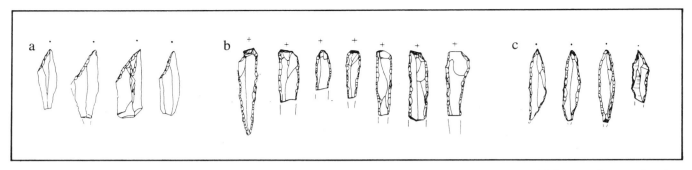

Nab Head, Pembrokeshire, microlithic worked flints: these were integral components of the hunting and fishing toolkits used in the Mesolithic period between c.7000 and 4000 BC. After R. M. Jacobi in Taylor 1980, with permission.

Carneddau Hengwm, Dyffryn Ardudwy, Meirionnydd: a pair of megalithic tombs, first noted by Edward Lhuyd during the 1690s and little changed since then. These collections of large fieldstones revetted by flat or boulder uprights, in which slab-covered stone chambers were set as receptacles for bones and grave goods, were communal graves of the Neolithic Period (c.4000-2500 BC). It is unusual to find paired tombs, and these belong to a group of over half a dozen single tombs known to have existed in this area. 93-cs-1014

Forests were burned or felled to make way for farming and new communities. Polished stone axes fashioned from virtually any available hard stone were put to service for felling and digging, hence the use of 'Neolithic' (New Stone Age) as the term to describe this period. Some workshops in upland Wales produced flaked axes which probably served local demands for tackling softwoods (Briggs 2003; Lynch 2000).

More sophisticated farming societies developed from the admixture of old and new husbandry practices. They buried their dead in collective monuments of considerable size - long barrows or megalithic tombs (Lynch 2000). Most tombs known from lowland areas were of earth or earth and stone covering regular interment chambers of stone or wood (Barker 1992). Upland collective tombs were usually megalithic (i.e. of big stones). They range from the large and visually spectacular to modest-sized monuments still partially earth-covered, like Mynydd Troed (Brecknocks)(RCAHMW 1997). Only one fresh discovery of this type has resulted directly from recent fieldwork in the uplands. Of simple upright stones, it was found near Lake Vyrnwy in 1993.

More typical examples with flagstone chambers and forecourts may remain covered in small boulders or field stones. Others, like Gwern Einion (Meirionnydd)(Bowen and Gresham 1967), Plas Newydd (Anglesey- not in the uplands) (RCAHMW 1937) and Pentre Ifan (Pembrokeshire)(Lynch 2000), completely stripped of their cairn mass can give an impression of free-standing architecture meant to impress the viewer. Indeed some people nowadays suppose that the tombs' gaunt stones were originally intended to be seen as picturesque monuments in what is actually now their half-built or dilapidated and denuded state.

Although a number of Neolithic graves are known from the margins of the Welsh uplands their relationships to forest

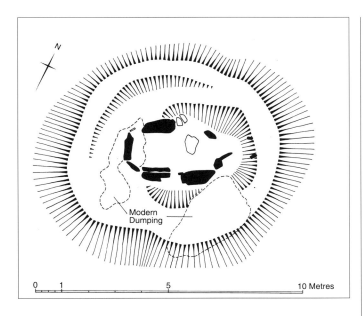

Plan of a megalithic structure, possibly a Neolithic tomb, near Lake Vyrnwy, Montgomeryshire. This was found by Richard Hankinson in the course of systematic fieldwork in the uplands of western Montgomeryshire. If excavation shows this to be truly a Neolithic tomb it will be the first such site to have been authenticated from the recent upland reconnaissance programmes. After fig. in Silvester 1994: 51.

and land clearances are imperfectly understood (Barker 1992; RCAHMW 1997). There are certainly many records of *landnam* (land taking) horizons in the upland forest pollen record between *c*.4,500 and 3,000 BC, but the degree to which field boundaries were used to regulate farming activity is at present conjectural. House sites from this period in Wales are extremely rare (Darvill and Thomas 1996).

The Early Bronze Age: Burial and Ritual Monuments

Farming traditions probably continued in the uplands until the end of the early Middle Bronze Age (*c*.1,200-1,000 BC). Although small amounts of copper, bronze or even gold were being increasingly used during this period, little is understood about the ways ores were collected (Briggs 2003). Metal artefacts and ornaments are few and far between in the uplands, though occasional personal adornments have been found among burial remains (Lynch 1993).

After *c*.2,500 BC the pollen record shows how farming made greater inroads into the woodlands on the higher ground in Wales. Weeds indicative of cultivation or animal husbandry have been detected. Moreover, evidence is mounting to suggest that an important outcome of inefficient husbandry was widespread soil acidification. Heathlands developed on

Cefn Sychbant, Cwm Cadlan, Brecknock: probable Bronze Age ring cairn. This is one of a number of cairns and cairn-like features, most of which appear to have been associated with agricultural clearance. This one seems to have been most likely for burial or ritual, though it is unclear whether or not it was built in this form or is the remnant of a much larger, robbed-out cairn. RCAHMW 1997: 97-8; C 81048

Maen Llia, Defynnog, Brecknock: a standing stone of uncertain status. It may be of prehistoric origin but later inscribed to commemorate the death of a local person of standing in immediately post-Roman times. There are some who doubt the authenticity and detail of the inscription. RCAHMW 1997: 170; C81021

these soils and impeded drainage caused the inception of widespread peat growth by about 1,200 -1,000 BC. Although peat growth also accompanied deteriorating weather conditions, it is unclear how far climate and vegetational changes were interdependent (Caseldine 1990). Cooling conditions may have been exacerbated by dust clouds from the volcanoes of Hekla and Santorini, which would have occluded the sun and shortened cropping seasons (Pilcher *et al.* 1996).

If analogies are drawn with landscapes surveyed in other parts of Britain, like Dartmoor and the Pennines, then some of the partial field boundaries and clearance areas surveyed in upland Wales (see chapter 3.4; Silvester 1992) probably represent permanent contemporary occupation in later prehistoric times (Briggs 1985; 1991a).

However, most evidence for human activity at this time has come from the survey and excavation of Early Bronze Age ritual and funerary monuments (e.g. Lynch 1993). These are among the strongest defining features of this period in the Welsh uplands (Lynch 2000). There are four main types: cairns, stone circles, stone rows and standing stones, all probably dating from *c.*2,200-1,000 BC. The most visible and common are burial cairns. They range from about 5 metres in diameter and one metre high to five or even ten times that in area with heights exceptionally over 5 metres. Many cairns are revetted by upstanding boulders or flat stones (Lynch 1972; Silvester 1992). Inside these monuments burials were usually placed centrally within stone chambers or cists. Many have been damaged by stone seekers, leaving only a cist or the encircling uprights free from cairn mass.

At one time circular monuments of free-standing stone uprights (stone circles) were considered to have been deliberately built and used for prehistoric ritual. Tradition adopted them as *Druids' Circles*. Nowadays most are regarded as the surviving stones of denuded or unfinished structured cairns.

Stone alignments are relatively rare. They can include as many as a dozen upright stones of up to half a metre high, exceptionally with stones over twice that height. Some could have been erected to make solar observations for predicting the seasons in the deteriorating climatic conditions of the second millennium B.C. Some may indicate the sites of land boundaries.

Today a huge number of upright stones and boulders can be seen in the Uplands. Virtually all are glacial erratics or naturally detached blocks. However, some were purposely raised to upstanding positions (Williams 1988; Hankinson *et al.* 1998; Sambrook & Hankinson, 2001). Although it has been shown that a few marked the sites of prehistoric burials or pits, many others certainly later acted as boundary markers. Most probably still lie in or close to positions where nature left them.

When, during the 1960s, it was suggested that some Early

Lle'r Neuaddau, Melindwr, Ceredigion: an Early Bronze Age kerb cairn. Over thirty of these cairns are known in mid-Wales. A mound of soil or boulders was revetted over an inhumation or cremation burial with grave goods placed in a cist or box. Stripped bare, they have often been mistaken for free-standing stone circles. The surrounding area was probably pitted with cremation burials. Private collection 1977

Fridd Bod y Fuddau, Trawsfynydd, Meirionnydd: a hut group on the southern slope of Cwm Prysor at 400 metres above sea-level. It is tempting to relate the narrow cultivation ridges which cover the adjacent area to the earlier or earliest occupation of the site. The date of the wider cultivation ridges beyond and their relationship to the 'narrow rig' is also uncertain. The rectangular enclosure is of unknown date. 91-cs-170

(opposite) Saeth Maen, Craig y Nos, Brecknock: a stone row, probably of the Early Bronze Age. Stone rows are enigmatic monuments found in various forms throughout the British Isles. It is unclear how much this example has been affected by interference from visitors. RCAHMW 1997: fig. 90; C 81030

Bronze Age monuments may have been built as sophisticated astronomical observatories (Thom 1967) their sitings became the subject of heated debate. However, the detailed surveys conducted to test this hypothesis at a number of sites, including one in Carmarthenshire, felt that it was unconvincing (Morgan and Ruggles 1976).

The Iron Age

Although the Uplands have not yielded a great deal of direct evidence to detail the type of settlement and farming carried on during the Bronze Age, a different perception exists of the Iron Age. Indeed, in North Wales a wide range of huts and hut-groups has survived which are believed to date from the later centuries BC (Kelly 1990; RCAHMW 1960; Silvester 1992). Their survival is more unusual in South Wales (RCAHMW 1997). A number of hut forms are known, mostly circular. Many are associated with enclosures which could have been animal pens, and with field boundaries, lynchets or even terraced ground obviously used for crop cultivation (Briggs 1985). Not many have been excavated, but significant organic evidence of crop types has been recognised at Cefn Graeanog, Caernarvonshire (Fasham *et al.* 1998).

By about 1000 BC large communal enclosures, later to become hillforts, were being built in more lowland parts of Britain (Avery 1993). Significant numbers skirt the remoter uplands, with a few penetrating their hinterland. Tre'r Ceiri (Musson 1994, 80-81) and Garn Boduan, Caernarvonshire (both RCAHMW 1964), and the Breiddin, Montgomeryshire (Musson *et al.* 1991), are among numerous fortresses of this type located within the upland province. The socio-economic and political relationships between these hillforts and nearby hut-groups have not yet been established to any great degree and little is known of contemporary burial practice (Whimster 1981).

Industrial sites for iron-working are being recognised in increasing numbers throughout Wales (Crew 1998).

Roman Activity

Not long after the Romans had invaded Britain (AD 43) and started to establish towns in the lowlands they began to conduct campaigns against the aboriginal groups of northern England and the several tribes inhabiting Wales (Arnold & Davies 2000). It is unclear how far they were motivated to conquer Wales to exploit minerals. They certainly recovered lead and copper from Welsh locations and may also have taken

Roman road north of Caersws, Montgomeryshire: one of the best-preserved Roman roads in Wales runs north from the fort at Caersws towards the Banwy valley and an unknown destination further north. 94-cs-0059

seventy years (Arnold & Davies 2000). Fresh discoveries of forts and camps from aerial photography were made during the 1960s and 70s, and aerial survey continues to provide important additions to the record today, sometimes as an adjunct to the Uplands Initiative (see the example of Tomen y Mur on pages 14 & 15 of this volume).

Some of the best-preserved Roman features in the uplands are marching camps and practice camps. Because these served more the role of overnight settlements in remote areas, once abandoned they were not changed by later occupation and can still be seen sharply defined in the landscape today. Esgair Perfedd marching camp was discovered on the ground by A. H. A. Hogg, a former secretary of the Royal Commission.

There is further monumental evidence of upland occupation in the early post-Roman period after the fifth century AD, when it is believed early Christian settlements were established near the roads. Indeed, some memorial stones, like the Maen Llia, Brecknock, are believed to have been erected in order to mark passes on difficult terrain.

How the Hills were settled: Pastoralists and Agriculturalists

It was at one time a commonplace teaching that during prehistoric times people lived only in the hills because the lowlands were boggy or afforested. It was also believed that the only sustainable farming activity in the hills was herding or pastoralism. So whilst intrepid early man was thought to have travelled and traded afar, driving his flocks or herds through remote highland passes or along the fastnessses of mountain ridges, conversely the lowlands were seen as impassable and uncultivable. These interpretations of past behaviour combined possibly long-lost traditions of husbandry with some of the realities of post-medieval economic pastoral practice and stock-breeding that were probably governed by quite different climatic regimes.

Such ideas were absorbed into the outlook of the newly-founded School of Geography at Aberystwyth under Professor H. J. Fleure between *c*.1915 and 1935. As a leading anthropologist one of Fleure's interests was in the endurance of social and economic tradition. So his promotion of this more pastoral interpretation of the Welsh uplands was informed by detailed understanding of recent pastoral traditions among European hill-dwellers as far afield as Spain and Switzerland.

Until Fleure's day the existence of ancient pastoral hill cultures had been supported on the grounds of differential

gold (Briggs 2003). However the case for Roman mining is not supported by the sort of evidence normally demanded to demonstrate the age of other types of site (Briggs 1991;1994a), so at present it seems most realistic to suppose they tapped deposits on or near the surface.

Whatever their motives for colonising Wales, the Romans engineered roads east-west cross-country towards the west coast and spinally north-south, with direct route alignments sometimes bravely tackling high passes or traversing plateaux over land in every sense hostile. To defend these routeways a series of forts was built at strategic locations. Most forts in the uplands are thought to have been used for not more than about

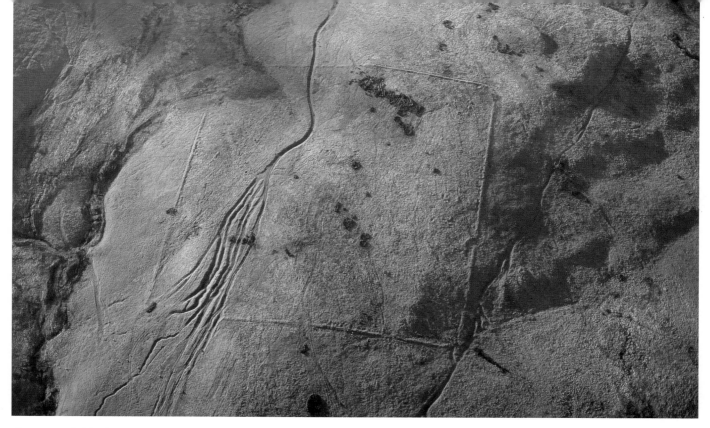

Esgair Perfedd, Rhayader, Radnorshire: a Roman marching camp, occupied by soldiers on campaign. The site was discovered from the ground by A. H. A. Hogg early in 1966. 98-cs-0954

topography and immutable tradition. This picture changed with Cyril Fox's *Personality of Britain* in 1932. Confronted by mapped distributions of prehistoric sites and finds showing that, contrary to the assumption that it had been uninhabitable, parts of lowland Britain appeared to have been well-populated during later prehistoric times, Fox produced a new theory of early settlement. Britain should be divided into Upland and Lowland Zones. Different environmental conditions would have governed the early settlement of each zone. This analysis was the first step towards a more critical evaluation of the settlement evidence. However, Fox's distribution maps hardly changed the notion that prehistoric people in Wales had occupied the hills rather than the valleys.

The simplicity of Fox's explanations has gradually come into question. Nowadays the results of widespread aerial photography demonstrate discontinuous settlement patterns covering most parts of Britain from coast to coast since the third millennium BC (Hampton and Palmer 1977). As well as burials and individual settlement sites, extensive early field patterns are also now known. Interpreting this palimpsest landscape is helped in the lowlands by cropmark distinctions between one type of field system and another (Musson 1994).

In spite of aerial discovery and settlement excavations which provided useful insights into prehistoric crop and animal husbandry, there was a general reluctance to look for or record early land divisions in the uplands which lasted at least until the 1970s. When Dartmoor was then mapped much of its surface was found to be still covered in co-axial field walls or boundaries considered to be of Bronze Age origin (Fleming 1989). In Wales, when field mapping in the Ardudwy area began, a whole new world of early settlement was revealed (Kelly 1982). Since then early field systems have been recorded in many parts of upland Wales in what are seen as zones of preservation (summarised in RCAHMW 1997). Interestingly, some antiquarians and local farmers had long known of these features without appreciating their importance to early agriculture and social organisation. Regular discoveries of fields and clearances are currently being made in the Uplands Initiative. These discoveries are among the most important contribution to an understanding of prehistoric life currently being made from field reconnaissance in the Welsh uplands.

UPLAND ARCHAEOLOGY IN THE MEDIEVAL AND POST-MEDIEVAL PERIODS

D. K. Leighton (Royal Commission on the Ancient and Historical Monuments of Wales) and R. J. Silvester (Clwyd-Powys Archaeological Trust)

Introduction

The first decade of the Uplands Initiative produced a huge increase in the number of recorded monuments that can be broadly ascribed to the medieval and post-medieval periods. Many of the sites fall into the very general categories of 'platform' and 'long-hut', together with their associated structures. However, the identification and study of these sites have highlighted the difficulties of matching them to the conventional historical subdivisions of the period, throwing into sharp focus issues of chronology and continuity across a time span of more than a millennium.

The period between the end of the Roman province, in the early fifth century AD, and the start of the nineteenth century saw immense political, social and economic changes: the breakdown of Roman provincial authority, the establishment of the church, the coming of the Normans, the decline in some areas – but its persistence in others – of native customary tenure, and the eventual union with England were accompanied by the effects of climate change and natural disaster. All these will have contributed to a greater or lesser degree to the archaeological record, but subdividing the period on the basis of the physical evidence alone and allocating that evidence accordingly has proved extremely difficult. To some extent the problem has been alleviated by the study of documentary sources in tandem with field survey where circumstances have allowed, and also by research conducted in parallel with, but separately from, the Uplands Initiative during the life of the project.

A traditional view that the uplands were essentially a detached wilderness abandoned save for brief, episodic pastoral activity – an impression easily conveyed by bleak moorland pasture scattered with building remains – is giving way to a more intricate picture commensurate with the convoluted historical background. Abandonment was a feature of land-use history in some areas at some times, but is unlikely to have been total in any single locality, while continuity and consolidation occurred elsewhere, perhaps with modified land-use regimes. Evidence for arable cultivation at high altitude in the historic period is now well documented, and links with surrounding lowlands are being emphasised.

Throughout the period climate change was sufficiently marked to influence human activity, particularly in upland areas (Parry 1985). However, recent research has cautioned against invoking this, or any other single factor, as a primary and independent cause of economic shift, with generalised implications for 'occupation' and 'abandonment', 'advance' and 'retreat' (Bell 1989; Dyer 1989). In sum the evidence shows that the ebb and flow of settlement and land use in the uplands during the historic period was a response to economic change. Nevertheless, non-economic factors, operating unevenly across the landscape, also influenced land use, giving rise to contrasts in site distribution and density. Furthermore, the impact of change, and therefore its reflection in the archaeological record, will have varied from one locality to another according to the ability of communities to respond and adapt to that change, whatever its nature (Bailey 1991).

The early medieval period

The early historic period was distinguished in macro-climatic terms by a sequence of short-term fluctuations. The amelioration of the climate in the Roman period gave way to decline, but with a trend towards drier and less stormy conditions and a general improvement from the seventh century onwards (Lamb 1981; Parry 1985). The limited evidence for upland vegetational history presents a mixed picture. The open environment at the end of the Roman period was followed by woodland regeneration in some areas, but continued openness and peat accumulation in others (Caseldine 1990, 94; Chambers 1983, 313). Historical sources and place-name evidence suggest that Snowdonia may have remained substantially wooded until well into the Middle Ages (Garnett & Richardson 1989). The lack of evidence for upland agricultural activity is consistent with contraction following the collapse of Roman central authority and recurrent outbreaks of plague (Davies 1982, 41-2). However, while pastoral activity ended in some localities (Caseldine 1990) it intensified in others (Lawler *et al.* 1997, 101).

(opposite) Cwm Nantcol: an upland valley in south-western Snowdonia, east of Llanbedr, showing the uphill advance of land improvements along the sheltered valley. 93-cs-1040

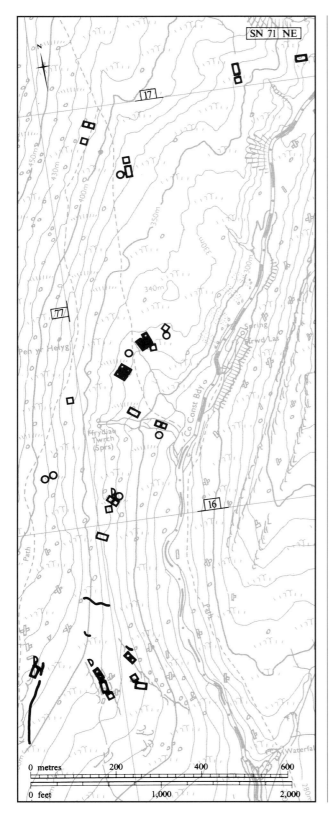

Of the sixteen known secular settlement sites with dates between the end of the Roman period and the Norman conquest (Edwards 2001, 15) none is located in the uplands. Several lie on the upland fringes, as for example Graeanog (Kelly 1990; Fasham *et al.* 1998). This offers circumstantial evidence for the use of adjacent high ground, as does the record of early church foundations, for example in the Tanat valley (Britnell 1994), at Gelligaer (RCAHMW 1976, 4, 44), and at Tregaron (Murphy 1999, 11) and other locations on the margins of upland Ceredigion (James 1994, 398, map). The principal material remains from the period – an assemblage of inscribed stones – also provide pointers to upland activity. These have a mostly lowland and westerly distribution, but a significant number of fifth - to sixth-century date are found in upland locations, notably in the north and south of the country. Some are believed to have been symbols of land ownership erected either by secular elites or by the church (Edwards 2001). In Glamorgan their distribution in the upper Taff valley may reflect a settlement pattern of farmsteads strategically placed to exploit a range of environments: streams, enclosed land and open moorland (Knight 1978). The limits of pasture may have been defined by systems of dykes traversing the ridges which are a feature of the Glamorgan uplands (RCAHMW 1976, 5); but associated settlement sites, if present, are elusive.

In North Wales late prehistoric or Romano-British hut circles are frequently associated with rectangular structures normally ascribed to later periods (Kelly 1990; Fasham *et al.* 1998, 84). The frequency with which they were built on, or otherwise respect, round huts, and sometimes were created through their modification, suggests that the one evolved from the other, perhaps initially as ancillary buildings and then as dwellings. The impression is of continuity, or at least of no major discontinuity, in both settlement and land use, with the re-use of field systems (Thompson 2000, 24). A looser relationship between rectangular buildings and open settlements has been noted on Mynydd Preseli (Sambrook & Ramsey 1998, 2), and palaeo-botanical indications for

---

Twrch Valley: long-huts and their ancillary structures often cluster in profusion like those illustrated in this example from Mynydd Du in south-eastern Carmarthenshire. A variety of structures is represented: rectangular buildings with and without partitions, enclosures of square, circular and semi-circular form, and short lengths of curvilinear walling. They all lie above the steep cutting of the Afon Twrch and close to streams which drain into it. Leighton 1997, Fig 54

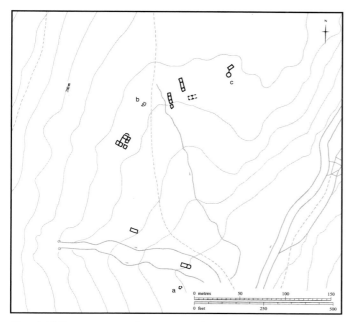

Twrch Valley: a group of structures close to mountain streams draining into the Afon Twrch in south-east Carmarthenshire. This nucleation features several rectangular buildings of varying complexity. Additionally there are two crudely built sub-circular pens, possibly intended for poultry or swine (a, b), and a larger circular fold (c). Leighton 1997, Fig 52

cultivation on Mynydd Du from the eighth century in the vicinity of rectangular buildings also hint at the potentially early beginnings of these structures outside North Wales (Leighton 1997, 99).

The later medieval period

The climatic warming which began in the seventh century culminated in an optimum between *c.*1150 and *c.*1250 AD, before decline again set in. Research elsewhere in Britain has shown that this 'high medieval' period saw the expansion of settlement and farming into the uplands (Parry 1985), stimulated by land hunger stemming from population growth. The process was further driven in Wales by the custom of *gavelkind*, or partible inheritance, the equal division of hereditary property among the heirs. This led to the fragmentation of holdings, which became less viable as economic units, so encouraging colonisation on to marginal lands. There is some evidence that the population of Wales was now more evenly dispersed across uplands and lowlands, with substantial numbers in some upland areas

(Davies 1987, 147).

The archaeological character of upland activity becomes clearer with the appearance of the 'classic' medieval type site – the rectangular platform built as a stance for a rectangular building, its long axis at right angles to the contour and cut into sloping ground, but showing little or no superficial trace of a building upon it. Recent survey has extended their distribution and revealed some regional contrasts. They are found in both uplands and lowlands, often in agricultural contexts. The excavated type site on Gelligaer Common in east Glamorgan, in the vicinity of cultivation ridges, produced dating evidence of the thirteenth and fourteenth centuries (Fox 1939; Locock 1999), but radiocarbon dates for sites like these are still lacking. Elsewhere in Glamorgan platforms are well known (RCAHMW 1982), and recent surveys have accentuated the existing distribution pattern (Locock 2000). However, they are poorly documented in Gwent, where less survey work has been done. They are known across the old county of Dyfed, though nowhere numerous, being most prevalent in north Carmarthenshire and south Ceredigion; they frequently show evidence for later re-use (Sambrook & Ramsey 1998, ix). In the Groes Fawr valley, east of Tregaron, some platforms are associated with cultivation ridges (Williams & Muckle 1992, 25).

Platforms are abundant in central Powys, where there are important groups in the Radnorshire district (Hankinson & Silvester 1997, 5.3). They extend into the north-west of the county and into south-west Denbighshire. However, to the north and east of this zone they occur only sporadically, if at all; they are sparsely represented in the Clwydian Hills, where Initiative surveys have uncovered relatively few sites of medieval date (Gale 1995, 12). Survey in the Berwyns identified a relict agricultural landscape with associated settlement extending above 400 metres above sea level in Cwm Pennant. Believed to represent expansion from the valley floor settlements, the platforms and their fields have survived in areas relatively unaffected by later land use (Silvester 2000). Platforms have been recorded widely across Gwynedd, where they usually support structural remains and are often overlain by later structures (Gresham 1954; Thompson 1998, *passim*). Survey in the Bwlch Mawr-Gyrn Goch area of Llyn, in particular, led to a marked increase in known platform sites (Geary 1998, 4.2).

This period of expansion coincided with the establishment of monastic houses. The Cistercian preference for remote areas attracted them to the uplands, where they were granted vast tracts by secular authorities for use as granges (Williams 1990, 91). Particularly large upland holdings were held by the

Hen Ddinbych: thought to be part of a monastic grange (farm) belonging to Denbigh Priory, the embanked enclosure known as Hen Ddinbych stands in a secluded position on the eastern side of the Brenig Valley; the disc-like feature off-centre is a reconstructed ring cairn. 91-cs-113

abbeys of Llantarnam (Monmouthshire), Strata Florida (Ceredigion), Cwmhir (Powys), Strata Marcella (Powys), Cymer (Gwynedd) and Aberconwy (Conwy). Grange activity may have extended to cultivation at altitude, for example in the enclosure attached to the hospitium above Lake Vyrnwy that belonged to the Knights Hospitallers (Silvester 1997). The eventual sale of the granges following the Dissolution in the mid-sixteenth century sometimes left a revealing documentary record. During the Mynydd y Ffynnon survey it was realised that holdings at the Cwmystwyth grange of Strata Florida were being leased to tenant farmers from the early 1500s, holdings which must have been established in the medieval period (Sambrook 1999, 10). Still identifiable, some were abandoned at an early date and survive as grassy platforms, while others functioned as farmsteads until well into the post-medieval period. These latter survive as rectilinear stone foundations, or 'long-huts', of varying complexity, and sometimes they are ruined upstanding buildings.

The arrival of the Anglo-Normans and English domination saw the expropriation of many upland areas for use as deer-parks and forests, exclusive preserves sometimes encompassing considerable areas. These seizures, together with the tendency of Marcher lords to impose demesne authority over pasture and other land resources (Davies 1978, 121), influenced settlement patterns, as illustrated by an example from the Brecon Beacons. Fforest Fawr in Cantref Mawr was established as a hunting preserve in the late eleventh century. Archaeologically, settlement here is characterised by platforms sometimes associated with arable farming. Such features are rare on neighbouring Mynydd Du, in Cantref Bychan, which remained outside Anglo-Norman jurisdiction for a further two centuries. The settlement evidence there is represented predominantly by long-huts, sometimes positioned on platforms, and their ancillary structures. These are comparatively rare on Fforest Fawr, where the enforcement of forest law limited access and subsequent settlement (Leighton 1997, 110). The distribution of remains in the Forest of Radnor reflected, in part, its function as a hunting preserve (Silvester 1992), and the sparseness of medieval settlement in the Clwydians may also be explained by demesne impositions there which included several deer-parks (Berry 1990; Gale 1995, 9).

Long-huts occur in large numbers across the Welsh uplands and contrast with the superficially unstructured platforms. The change to a greater use of stone may have been prompted initially by a shortage of timber, which was hastened from the thirteenth century onwards by worsening climate and the need to raise perishable materials on stone footings. Although some are supported by platforms many long-huts have different types of location to the grassy platforms already described, often on level ground and close to streams in sheltered valleys. These have been linked to the practice of transhumance or the seasonal movement of stock from the home farm (*hendre*) to the upland station (*hafod*), a function

Elan Valley Long-hut: this long-hut is located on the banks of a tributary stream of the Afon Elan, west of Rhayader. The foundations of buildings like this are found widely throughout the uplands of Wales and constitute one of the most frequently encountered monument types. This example, which incorporates a partition wall, has overall dimensions of 13 metres by 5 metres. NPRN 261621

which some of the platforms may also have served. Indeed, thirteenth-century references in the Welsh Laws imply that the *hafod* was then of light construction (Allen in Lynch 1993, 179). Long-huts discovered in the course of Uplands Initiative surveys are sometimes interpreted as former *hafotai* (e.g. Muckle 1996, 4). However, they are also known in the context of permanent settlement at relatively high altitude associated with cultivation, for example in Cwm Eigiau, at 385 metres above sea-level (RCAHMW 1956, 34, no.163), and in Llŷn long-huts are associated with field systems (Geary 1998, 4.2). Some long-huts may have evolved into permanent farmsteads and components of the modern enclosure pattern as is suggested by the widespread prevalence of farms with the *hafod* element in their names.

The climatic reversal which set in during the early fourteenth century was accompanied by animal disease, famine and plague. Depopulation and economic downturn will have affected upland habitation, causing the shrinkage and even desertion of some settlements. Land-use practices changed as arable cultivation at altitude became less viable. Moreover, at the same time native customs of inheritance were being dismantled and replaced by English forms of land tenure. This encouraged the growth of single consolidated farmsteads as the custom of partible inheritance declined.

Craig Cerrig-gleisiad: the foundations of a partitioned rectangular building, set within an enclosure, are located below the cliffs of Craig Cerrig-gleisiad on the northern escarpment of Fforest Fawr. The valley is richly endowed with archaeological remains, the walls of the glacial cwm having offered protection for early settlement over a long period of time. 2001-cs-0508

Detailed local studies are beginning to reveal the complexity of the late medieval settlement pattern. For example, on higher ground in the Conwy Valley long-huts and their associated field systems are overlain by later holdings. A period of cultivation and occupation, probably of thirteenth century date, was followed by abandonment and re-use for summer pasture which was in turn re-occupied as improving climate and new inheritance laws encouraged expansion during the later fifteenth century and after. The disconformity in the layouts of the two field systems reflects the changed economic and social circumstances (Hooke 1997; Thompson 1998).

The post-medieval landscape

It is widely recognised by archaeologists that the closer we get to the present day, the more prevalent become the archaeological remains. This is as true for the uplands as it is for other areas. Equally, we should recognise that those remains are more diverse in their appearance and function than their medieval predecessors.

This trend is reflected strongly in many, if not all, of the field surveys that have been conducted over the last ten years under the aegis of the Uplands Initiative. Pastoralism and agriculture, enclosure, settlement, subsistence, industry and leisure are all represented in the record. Industry is considered elsewhere in this volume, but here we examine these other activities.

A high degree of continuity from the Middle Ages into later centuries is only to be expected. Although platform sites are known to have continued in use and to have been constructed after the medieval era, evidence is also emerging for more complex types of settlement which may reflect the reappearance of farm steadings in the hills after the disasters of the fourteenth century. Earthworks comprising building platforms encased in complex patterns of enclosures and small fields have been

The upland hamlet of Moelfre City, lying just north of Llanbister in upland Radnorshire. In the left foreground is the recently scheduled deserted rural settlement on Moelfre Hill, a farmstead with an outer enclosure and a well-defined house platform within. To the right of the photograph can be seen comparatively late- 18th- and 19th-century encroachment of farms and fields onto the high common. The preservation of this pattern of squatters' settlement at Moelfre is of particular interset. RCAHMW. 2001/3503-34

identified just inside the boundaries of several commons in central Powys, as at Moelfre City and on Fron Top, both in Llanbister. There is little independent dating evidence, but the excavated site at Beili Bedw, St Harmon (Courtney 1991), shows a similar farmstead succeeding a platform settlement, and there are slight indications that the latter may have been in use about the late sixteenth or early seventeenth century.

The number of these, though, is very small when compared with the expansion of settlement that was to come. Farms developed where enclosed land met open upland, perhaps the result of individual farming families expanding their holdings. Moreover, from the later seventeenth century through to the nineteenth century increasing numbers of the rural poor attempted to generate a living for themselves by moving on to the commons and wastes. Building small, flimsy structures, known as *tai unnos*, or one-night houses, they enclosed small plots of land around them. Where successful the cottages were subsequently replaced by more permanent structures; some have remained inhabited up to the present day, but many others have been abandoned, and the remains of these encroachments are a frequently encountered element of upland surveys.

Typical is the situation recorded around Cefn Cyfarwydd, west of the Conwy in north-west Wales, in a survey of 1993-4, where the valley edging the west side of the mountain had been largely abandoned by the 1930s, leaving five farmhouses and cottages with their ancillary buildings and the Siglen Methodist chapel, all in ruins (Carver *et al.* 1994). One of the earliest surveys conducted under the Initiative was in the enclosed hills to the north of Newtown (Montgomeryshire), centred on a holding called Carneddau, where of sixteen farmhouses functioning in the nineteenth century ten had been abandoned by the time of the study (Silvester 1990).

Not all settlement in these later centuries was permanent. Seasonal use of the upland pastures continued and lasted longer in some of the more westerly parts of Wales. Leland in the 1530s observed cottages in upland Cardiganshire occupied seasonally as summer dairies (Sambrook and Ramsey 1998, 34), while travellers such as Thomas Pennant commented on seasonal activity in the mountains of Caernarvonshire at the end of the eighteenth century; it has recently been documented even in early-twentieth-century Snowdonia (Thompson 1997, 15). Many of the stone-built long-huts found in remote upland valleys are likely to date from the post-medieval centuries, and some of the surveys have distinguished remarkable numbers of such sites. Much of the mountainous area of Gwynedd, for instance, remains unknown archaeologically. When Peter Muckle surveyed Moel Llechwedd-gwyn, a few miles to the

east of Ffestiniog, in 1995, not a single archaeological site had been previously recorded in the six square kilometres that he examined. Yet fieldwork revealed eighteen certain and five possible long-huts, together with five other habitations where the state of the building suggested more recent occupation in perhaps the eighteenth and nineteenth centuries (Muckle 1996, 4). Less common are specific concentrations of such sites, so the occurrence of several such groups in the Elan Valley area of western Powys is worth noting. It is one of the achievements of the fieldwork programme that cumulatively very large numbers of such sites have been identified, and it is not simply the long-huts themselves that are revealed, but also the features associated with them. Evidence in the form of small nearby cairns, indicative of small-scale ground clearance to facilitate cultivation plots, has come from Mynydd Mallaen in Carmarthenshire (Williams and Darke 1996), and possible middens have been identified in upland Ceredigion (Williams and Muckle 1992).

Farming on the commons and the waste has left extensive traces in the uplands. Sheep farming has, of course, dominated the economy of many uplands in recent centuries, but tangible signs of this activity are restricted to shepherds' huts and shelters, sheepfolds, washing pools and shelter walls. However, there are also field and enclosure boundaries which show as banks or walls and, in slate-quarrying areas such as around Moel Bowydd to the north-east of Ffestiniog (Hopewell 2000), as slate fences where narrow slate slabs up to 1.5 metres high are set side by side to create long boundaries running over the hills. Past farming practices are also indicated by cairns from the clearance of stone, the ruins of barns or sometimes simply their stances, and traces, too, of cultivation in the form of narrow ridges, where crops were grown on the open mountain land and then the ground abandoned.

More specialised activities also took place, one being the breeding of rabbits in small warrens. Earthworks known as pillow mounds were specially constructed, often with deliberately fashioned burrows, and these are not infrequently encountered. The remains of forty such warrens with the pillow mound numbers ranging from one to a dozen have been recognised in the Radnorshire district of Powys (Silvester forthcoming b), many of them on the open uplands. In some places in the Brecon Beacons warrening took place on what can only be considered an 'industrial' level in the nineteenth century (Leighton 1997, 42).

The uplands provided other resources that could also be harvested: fern, gorse and kindling. Most of these activities leave no discernible traces, but what was probably the most

Llwyn-du Parc: a complex of nineteenth-century sheepfolds with encroaching forestry, east of Dyffryn Ardudwy. Sheep were once the primary dairy animal and thus needed to be more actively herded and controlled than their modern counterparts. This gave rise to a variety of structures designed for managing flocks on the open hillside, some of considerable complexity. Most, like these, became disused and ruinous as methods of sheep management changed. 93-cs-1007

extensive subsistence industry is apparent in the landscape. Peat was for many the major and often the only fuel, particularly in the post-medieval centuries. Individual farms and whole communities worked the peat beds or turbaries, and the linear cuttings can still be recognised, particularly from the air. An impressive area of peat workings with trackways leading to it was noted in the final season at Mynydd y Ffynnon (Sambrook 2001). Mounds of peat that was never collected and the platforms on which the peat was stacked can

be identified in some areas, as around Corlan Fraith, where rectangular platforms of large stones have been recorded. In upland Montgomeryshire earthen rectangular platforms with surrounding gullies were constructed; one excavated at Carneddau near Newtown had had upright timbers around it to protect the drying peat from being knocked over by stock. Frequent use of the same turbaries, often on high and remote plateaux, led to problems of access, and where steep slopes had to be negotiated, often by sled, the difficult conditions led

Rhos Saith-maen: peat-cutting features, sharply etched under light snow, at more than 400 metres above sea-level. The well-ordered character of these cuttings suggests a fairly recent date, though the exploitation of peat deposits (turbaries) has a long history. 96-cs-0292

to the formation of numerous paths, which have been termed braided trackways.

Quarrying was carried out on an extensive scale in many upland areas, both commercially and to provide the raw material for buildings, walls and the like. One survey in the Black Mountains of eastern Brecknock identified over 120 quarries, around 30 per cent of the total number of sites recognised (Hankinson *et al.* 1998, 5).

Trackways were, of course, fundamental to activities other than peat cutting, and some may even have had their origin in the prehistoric era. Tracks of one form or another can link settlements or isolated farms, run from farmsteads to outlying fields or to the open grazing, and serve quarries. Numerous trackways carried traffic over the Clwydian hills from the Vale of Clwyd to the lowlands further east (DCC 1998).

The uplands also display other linear features such as leats. These may have had an industrial function, taking water from an upland stream or lake to mines or quarries, but they could also serve farms, and may run for long distances. Upright stones as well as other features, some natural, were used to mark boundaries. A line of stones on Mynydd Uchaf in western Glamorgan was inscribed 'C G n', defining the southern boundary of the Manor of Caegurwen (Yates 1998, 7).

The hills have been used for leisure for many centuries. Hunting was a medieval pursuit that certainly continued into later times, but it is shooting that leaves tangible remains.

Some estates have used specific commons for grouse shooting for generations, and in the second half of the nineteenth century this became more common and shooting hides or butts were constructed for the sportsmen. Some open uplands have large numbers of such butts; the limestone plateaux north of the Dee Valley were and still are used extensively for shooting, and butts are commonplace, while well over one hundred have been recorded on Llanbedr and Glascwm Hills, one of the Radnorshire Commons. More rarely buildings reflect sporting interest, such as the 'Bird House' on the summit of Mynydd Maen near Cwmbran, now destroyed (Locock 1997, 11).

Mynydd Cil-cwm: a complex of braided trackways, probably related to peat-cutting activities of long duration, ascend Mynydd Cil-cwm, near Llanbrynmair, at an altitude of 500 metres above sea-level. Tracks like these are usually determined by the topography they traverse – as one track becomes no longer usable a new line is chosen. 92-cs-1631

Military activity is also evidenced, and inevitably on somewhere like Mynydd Epynt, where the ranges are still in use, the remains of this activity, whether they be shell holes, targets or trenches, are extensive. In Cwm Llwch in the Brecon Beacons a newly identified rifle range is known to have been in use in 1900 (Skeates 1997, 39). Around Corlan Fraith (Meirionnydd) trenches, weapon pits and foxholes reflect activity at the time of World War II, and amongst the archaeological sites on Ruabon Mountain was a brick-and-concrete observation post with bunkers. Less usual military remains occur elsewhere, such as the Brecon rifle volunteers' camp on Gwernyfed Common, in the Black Mountains (Dorling 1994); the Reverend Francis Kilvert referred in his diary to a visit to the annual camp there in 1871, and five years later exceptionally heavy summer rain necessitated the construction of drainage gullies around the tents, nearly fifty of these small circular gullies still being visible.

A recurrent feature of the surveys has been the re-use of both settlement and burial sites at a later date and for different purposes. Essentially this was a practical matter, the earlier site providing some or perhaps all of the raw material for its successor. Medieval settlements adopted the sites of their prehistoric predecessors as we have noted above. The Cadair Idris survey identified two long-huts of medieval or early post-medieval date which showed simply as platforms protruding from beneath sheepfolds (GAT 1996, 9); on the western side of the Berwyn the sheepfold builders had a particular penchant for prehistoric burial cairns, and both a ring cairn and a large cairn with a cist in it were so utilised, the capstone of the cairn being left as an immovable object when the sheepfold builders rearranged the cairn material.

All these activities have left physical remains in the hills, though some more so than others. Not everything is immediately interpretable. A small earthwork about Lake Vyrnwy consists of a rectangular platform with a uninterrupted gully completely surrounding it. We still have no clear idea what the function of this small feature was.

We should remember that the uplands of Wales are infinitely varied. Different communities and individuals have used their own uplands in different ways over time, though influenced by the altitude, the remoteness, the climate and above all the nature of the landscape. This can be seen in the physical remains that have been left to us. To understand how man in the past has operated in the landscape we need to look beyond what might be classed as a global picture and instead consider and appreciate past activity at a local level. The spread of surveys across Wales funded under the Uplands Initiative takes us in the right direction.

INDUSTRIAL ACTIVITY

Stephen Hughes (Royal Commission on the Ancient and Historical Monuments of Wales) and Simon Timberlake (Archaeological Consultant)

A review of the first ten years of the results of the Uplands Initiative has shown that one of the two most common types of sites in these areas was extractive sites for metals, minerals and stone – the other being upland dwellings such as long-huts. Interestingly, the minerals required to fuel what became the largest ironworks in the world in the first half of the nineteenth century were sited in the uplands of south-eastern Wales. This importance has now been recognised by the World Heritage Landscape designation of the Blaenafon uplands. Much of the uplands of mid- and north Wales were also intensively mined for metals other than iron over a very long period. This was an economic activity that helped to create and maintain a sizeable population on the fringes of the uplands until the first half of the twentieth century.

Non-ferrous Metal Mines

It is apparent that a number of the largest and most famous of Welsh metal mines (e.g. Parys Mountain, Anglesey and Cwmystwyth, Ceredigion (Sambrook and Hankinson 2001)), as well as many other smaller mines and trial workings, have histories going back almost 4000 years to the very beginning of the metal-working period. However, most of these mines were at work during the nineteenth century, in particular during the boom years of metal mining between the 1860s and 1880s. Indeed, the upland zone between the 200- and 400-metre contours appears to have been the most intensively prospected area within Wales from the very beginning of the metal-using period (2000 BC) up to the decline of British metal mining in *c.*1900.

About three-quarters of the eight hundred and one non-ferrous mines were within the upland areas (i.e. over 200 metres) and primarily worked for lead and zinc. Not inconsiderable amounts of silver were also produced within certain parts of particular lead ore-fields, such as in south Ceredigion at Llanfair Clydogau, north Ceredigion north of the Rheidol, Llangynog in Powys (Montgomeryshire), Halkyn Mountain (Mynydd Helygain) in Flintshire and Minera by Wrexham. Occasionally, small amounts of gold were also extracted. A great many previously successful lead mines were re-worked on a large scale for zinc during the 1890s and the

first decade of the twentieth century, as at Frongoch and Cwmystwyth in upland north Ceredigion, Fan near Llanidloes, Powys, Halkyn Mountain (Mynydd Helygain) and Minera (Mwynglawdd) in north-east Wales.

Many lead mines also produced copper, but copper mines also formed an important class of their own within central Snowdonia and the Ganllwyd/Coed y Brenin area to the south. Mines producing gold and manganese were next in number and were sited in the Rhinog and Arenig Mountains, respectively north of Dolgellau and on the Llŷn Peninsula. Many of those sites recorded as gold mines were primarily prospecting trial mines, which produced little if any metal, the main productive mines being Prince Edward at Trawsfynydd and Gwynfynydd, Glogau, Vigra, Glasdir in the Dolgellau/Ganllwyd area, and Dolaucothi in Carmarthenshire.

The non-ferrous metal mines mentioned above are found in concentrations throughout upland Wales, whereas the distribution of coal and associated iron-mines was localised mainly to lowland areas of south and north-eastern Wales, but did extend onto the adjoining uplands of those relatively limited areas. However, of the more widely spread non-ferrous mines there are no less than one thousand seven hundred and forty-three metalliferous working or trial mines recorded for Wales. Some one thousand and eighty-three (62 per cent) of these are located within the upland zone.

The greatest concentration of upland non-ferrous metal mining in Wales (43 per cent) is somewhat unsurprisingly found in eastern Wales, where most of the area is upland. Over three-quarters of the mines of Powys, Flintshire and Denbighshire (four hundred and sixty-seven sites) are sited over 200 metres. The mostly upland area of north-western Wales (the old county of Gwynedd) has about a quarter of the upland mine sites in Wales, and 60 per cent (two hundred and fifty-eight mines) of its sites are located over 200m. The largely lowland area of south-western Wales (the former area of Dyfed) has two-thirds of its mines (two hundred and fifty-eight sites or 23.8 per cent of all upland Welsh sites) in the mineral rich upland area of north Ceredigion. The mostly lowland area of Glamorgan and Gwent has only twelve upland non-ferrous metals mines.

In recent years one of the most noteworthy discoveries has

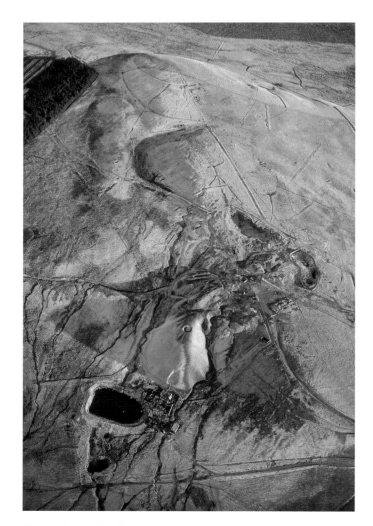

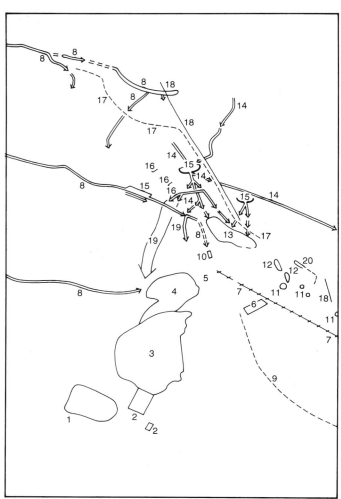

Esgair-Mwyn Lead mine: 99-cs-0242

1. Twentieth-century reservoir. 2. Remains of unused twentieth-century ore-concentrating mill and store. 3. Fine-ground waste-tip from nineteenth-century ore-concentrating mill. 4. Coarse waste-tip from nineteenth-century ore-concentrating mill. 5. Site of nineteenth-century ore-concentrating mill. 6. Ruins of nineteenth-century smithy. 7. Railway incline from nineteenth-century mine-shaft to mill. 8. Nineteenth- and twentieth-century water-power channels (leats). 9. Road to take lead ore towards Aberystwyth harbour for shipment to a smelting works. 10. Nineteenth-century waterwheel pit. 11. Mine shafts. 12. Collapsed top of deep workings on the mineral vein. 13. Opencast workings: possibly of prehistoric origin. 14. Scouring (hushing) watercourses: some described as 'old' in 1753, and possibly of considerable age. 15. Former water-storage reservoirs. 16. Prospecting trenches across the mineral vein. 17. Cart-track. 18. Boundary banks. 19. Water-scouring (hushing) channels. 20. Mining tunnel or trench.

been the great age of many of these early workings. Up to sixty (5.5 per cent) of the upland mines have probable 'early workings' (Bronze Age, Iron Age, Roman or Medieval) associated with them, although only a few of these (less than five) have not been worked since. Some 58 per cent of all 'early mines' lie within the upland zone. The survival of these, as well as many other later 'early workings', including those within the more remote upland areas, appears altogether more common than once thought. They remain either as open and partially peat/scree-infilled workings upon the higher outcrops of veins (Sambrook and Darke 1997), or are preserved intact beneath successive layers of tipping. Needless to say, much of

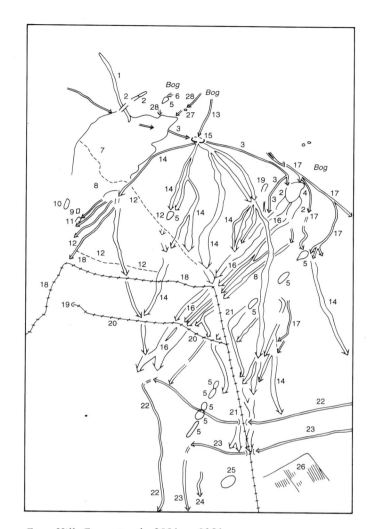

Copa Hill, Cwmystwyth: 2001-cs-0351

1. Exposed rock outcrop. 2. Early trenching (rake) on Kingside Mineral Vein. 3. Medieval water-supply channel to Comet Vein hushes. 4. Bronze Age opencast pit on the Comet Mineral Vein. 5. Other opencast pits. 6. Water-scouring (hushing) dams, possibly seventeenth century. 7. Kingside Vein dressing floors. 8. Waste and hushing from the Kingside Vein. 9. Mine Adventurers' water-powered stamping-mill of 1699. 10. Morgan Herbert's Stope of 1700: surface opening of deep underground workings. 11. Bonsall's mining tunnel (adit): eighteenth century. 12. Miners' tracks to Kingside Vein Workings: eighteenth century or earlier. 13. Water-supply channel to probably eighteenth-century hushing pond. 14. Hushing or scouring channels: probably eighteenth century. 15. Water-scouring reservoir: probably eighteenth century. 16. Medieval scouring on the Comet Mineral Vein. 17. Water-supply channels for scouring, and peat-sledge tracks. 18. Mineral railway to Pengeulan Mining Tunnel. 19. Mining tunnel. 20. Mineral railway to mining tunnel. 21. Railway inclined-plane formation. 22. Large water-power watercourse (leat) from the main Afon Ystwyth: mid-nineteenth century. 23. Smaller watercourse. 24. Eighteenth-century watercourse from the Nant-yr-Onnen. 25. Pengeulan mine-shaft. 26. Embanked field with cultivation ridges. 27. Mine-shafts. 28. Water-supply watercourses for scouring on the Kingside Mineral Vein.

the archaeological evidence for early exploitation upon rich lode outcrops will probably have been removed

Nevertheless, most of these relatively early mining features cannot be ascribed with any certainty to a particular period, even though relative 'earlier' and 'later' typologies can sometimes be identified on the basis of various chronological and technological markers. For example, the latest use of hammer stones as mining implements is unknown, even though there is no confirmed use beyond the prehistoric period within the British Isles (Timberlake 1992), and the last recorded or dateable use of the very long established practice of fire-setting within mines seems to be as late as 1730 in Flintshire (Lewis 1967).

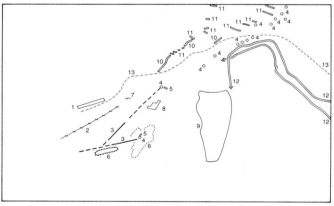

Esgairhir Lead and Copper Mines: 92-cs-1486

1. Ruins of mine offices. 2. Mineral railway from Esgairfraith Mine to ore-bins. 3. Line of pumping-rods from waterwheel to mine-shafts. 4. Mine-shafts: seventeenth century at top; nineteenth century at bottom. 5. Masonry pits to house counterbalance weights for pumping-rods. 6. Spoil from mine-shaft. 7. Ore-bins. 8. Ore-crushing and dressing-machinery house. 9. Water-supply reservoir for waterwheels. 10. Trench workings along the outcrop of the mineral vein: probably early. 11. Prospection trenches across the mineral veins: possibly seventeenth century. 12. Water-power supply channels (leats): probably eighteenth and nineteenth centuries. 13. Cart road constructed towards the port of Aberystwyth: mid-nineteenth century.

Within Wales forty-four sites (either mines , trial mines, or those within the proximity of such workings) have been identified from which hammer stones have been recorded. Many of these are isolated or uncorroborated finds, and for some it is uncertain whether the hammers fit the description of the utilised but barely modified cobble stones typical of Bronze Age mining. However, at least eleven sites (including four on the Great Orme) have been archaeologically excavated and have returned Bronze Age dates, most of which suggest a principal period of activity during the Early Bronze Age (2000 -1500 BC) (Timberlake, 2001), with the latest use of such technology extending up into the Late Bronze Age, or possibly into the Early Iron Age on the Great Orme (Lewis 1996). Furthermore, recent fieldwork has confirmed the presence of these mining hammers (occasionally in abundance), together with primitive mine-workings, at thirteen other sites. Most of these are located within the upland zone, mainly within mid-Wales. Seventeen of these are in north Ceredigion: Llancynfelin, Dolclettwr, Llainhir, Erglodd, Penpompren, Allt y Crib, Twll y Mwyn, Darren, Esgairhir, Esgairlle, Hafan/Hefnwlch, Nantycria, Nantyrarian, Grogwynion, Tyn y Fron, Rhiwurgos, Copa Hill (Cwmystwyth). Six are in Montgomeryshire (north Powys): Llangynog (Cwm Orog), Llangynog (Rock Level Opencut), Ogof Wyddon (Machynlleth), Nantyreira, Nantyrickets, Llanymynech. Three are in Merionydd (southern Gwynedd): Dinas Mawddwy, Balkan Hill and Panteidal (Aberdyfi). Two are further south: Pen Cerrig y Mwyn (Carmarthenshire) and All Slade Mine (Gower). Another fifteen sites are in north Wales, including Pant y Gaseg and Mynydd Parys on Anglesey (Ynys Mon), and six sites on the Great Orme (Penygogarth) at Llandudno, including Pyllau Valley (Vivian's/ Treweeks), Roman Shaft (summit), Ogof Tudno, Ffynnon Rufeiniog, Ffynnon Galchog and Pen Trwyn. Another five are in northern Gwynedd (the former Caernarfonshire) at Trecastell, Pen y Gaer (Abersoch), Bwlch y Plwm, Cwm Pennant Valley and Glaslyn. In Denbighshire and Flintshire are the two mines of Wagstaff Lead Vein (Halkyn/Helygain) and Craig y Forwen (Llangollen),

It is not usually possible on the surface to distinguish between examples of pre-Roman, Roman, medieval or sixteenth-century opencast trenches, although the presence of infilled small shafts and shaft mounds along the course of the untrenched vein differentiates medieval from earlier examples. Long rakes of the medieval period, probably extracting lead, are typical of early workings in limestone-hosted rocks (such as on Halkyn Mountain (Mynydd Helygain), Flintshire (Silvester and

Hankinson 1995), or on Hope (Yr Hob) or Esclusham Mountain, Denbighshire), and medieval or earlier examples were often not widened beyond the width of mineral taken out (sometimes as little as a few metres). In some cases the course of the rakes is barely recognisable today from the width of cutting, but more from the disturbance (uneven ground) resulting from the shallow spoil mounds, now heavily turf-covered. Most shafts associated with these early rakes (as shaft mounds) are probably later developments. Arcane names and location of sites within the ore fields (such as Pen y Bal, Holywell (Treffynnon) and Hope (Yr Hob) on Halkyn Mountain (Mynydd Helygain)) provide supporting evidence for mines of this period, and, loosely, these workings can be dated to the period AD 1280-1400. Particularly good examples are Wagstaff Rake and Long Rake (Halkyn Mountain).

Water-scouring (hushing) is the removal of the topsoil by the periodic release of stored water. It was practised in Wales from the Roman period at the Dolaucothi gold mines (Jones 1960; Cauuet *et al.* 2000), and perhaps also within other lead and gold mining areas. There are similar rectangular hushing tanks at Craig y Mwyn lead mine (Bick 1990), and radiocarbon dates have been obtained from long-silted channels that suggest a Roman date for hushing leats at Pen Cerrig y Mwyn (near Llandovery/Llanymddyfri: AD 460-480) and probably at Dylife (near Machynlleth: AD 980-1170, adjacent to Penycrocbren Roman fortlet (Timberlake 2002). There are very few references to hushing being practised. However, at Craig y Mwyn, Henry Hennings of the Powis Mines (Llangynog) is said to have carried out considerable work there from 1745 onwards in an attempt to discover the lost vein (Lewis 1967). If so, at least some of the hushing evidence above Craig y Mwyn may date from this period, although radiocarbon dates suggest an early-medieval date for a large part of this work (AD 1300-1460; Timberlake 2002). Several of the small crescent-shaped dams and ponds located above the opencast appear to have been used to assist mining, or else for the clearance of accumulated detritus. The evidence for hushing at Cwmystwyth is a radiocarbon date of *c.*AD 1450-68 for the older hushing leat along the crest of Copa Hill and documentary evidence at the end of the eighteenth century. The sequence of hushes (release channels) leading into the top edges of the Graig Fawr (probably used to assist in breaking up rock and ore, and also for removing accumulated detritus from the foot of the worked cliff-face) may also date from the first half of the eighteenth century or earlier (Hughes, S. R. 1994). This system of channels, supplied by a leat from a continuous water supply rather than hushing

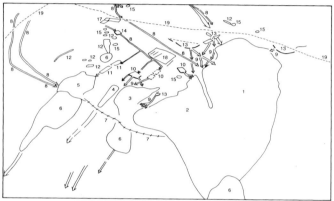

Craig y Mwyn Lead Mine: 93-cs-0834

1. Large opencast pit of early-medieval use. 2. Opencast pit of possible Roman origin and medieval re-use. 3. Opencast pit of possible Roman origin. 4. Opencast pit of possible Roman origin. 5. Opencast pit of possible Roman origin and nineteenth-century re-use. 6. Spoil heaps from opencast pits. 7. Mine railway formation: nineteenth century. 8. Artificial water-supply channels (leats). 9. Water-scouring (hushing) channels. 10. Rectangular water-tanks or reservoirs of Roman type. 11. Trial diggings or possible water-tanks. 12. Trial diggings and trenches. 13. Irregular water reservoirs of probable medieval date. 14. Rectangular water-control tank of Roman type. 15. Mine-shafts. 16. Ruins of 1740 smithy built across hushing channel. 17. House and garden. 18. Enclosed garden with cultivation ridges. 19. Modern farm-road.

tanks or ponds, shows evidence for repeated use and re-use, with water being diverted, and release channel breaches being blocked with stone dams. Particularly good examples of hushing are Craig y Mwyn, Graig Fawr (Cwmystwyth) and Esgair Mwyn.

Twenty-four (2.2 per cent) mines are known to have been at work during the sixteenth or seventeenth centuries and at least one hundred and seventy (16 per cent) have documentary reference for eighteenth-century working. Mines of this period are distinguished from earlier examples by the use of powder for blasting and driving levels or shafts. Powder was possibly used as early as 1692 at Llanymynech (Montgomeryshire/Powys, Shropshire border), but certainly by 1705 at Esgair Hir (north Ceredigion) and 1706 at Llanrhaiadr ym Mochnant (Montgomeryshire/Powys: Bick 1976 and 1978).

The use of some 'water engines' was recorded from 1700, but the widespread use of waterpower for pumping follows the general introduction of overshot waterwheels in the early years of the nineteenth century on upland sites (Bick 1993)).

There are numerous other technological markers for the later date of mining remains, including the introduction of tramways and gravity-fed dressing floors at some of the larger mines by the late 1840s (as one of many innovations brought in as a result of the adoption of Cornish mining methods). In addition, there are many other ways of recognising those distinctive styles of working which appear to be most characteristic of the seventeenth, eighteenth or even early nineteenth centuries. The latter may include factors such as the position and frequency of shafts, and the location, morphology and composition of spoil tips (Jenkins and Timberlake 1977).

After 1830 there was a significant period of change in the industry, including the introduction of modern capitalistic mining practices, technologically comparable machinery, and the adoption of more organised and streamlined designs for

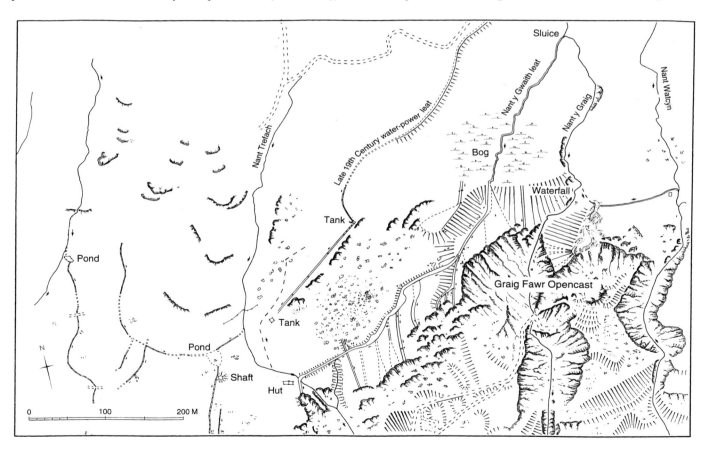

Cwmystwyth Lead Mine Hushing Channels: upland lead and silver mines often have the remains of water channels and storage ponds on the hillside above them, from which water was periodically released to scour or 'hush' the hillside below and so reveal the underlying strata and minerals. Such features can date from the Roman period to the late eighteenth century. At Cwmystwyth several artificial watercourses ('leats') such as the Nant y Gwaith ('Mine or Works Stream') and its release channels over the 340-metre-high lip of the Ystwyth Gorge were observed still in use in 1788. RCAHMW

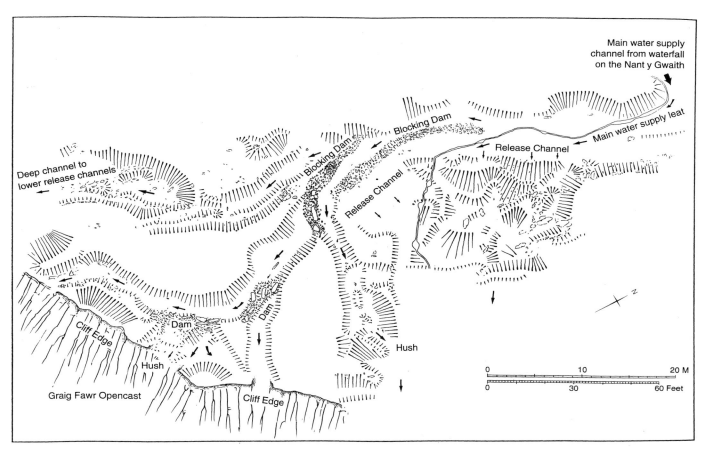

Main water supply
channel from waterfall
on the Nant y Gwaith

Main water supply leat

Blocking Dam

Blocking Dam

Release Channel

Release Channel

Deep channel to
lower release channels

Dam

Dam

Hush

Cliff Edge

Hush

Graig Fawr Opencast

Cliff Edge

Hush

N

0   10   20 M
0   30   60 Feet

Graig Fawr Hushing Dams: on the summit of the great rock that forms the northern edge of the Graig Fawr opencast mine at Cwmystwyth are the earthworks of a series of successive channels that guided water over the precipitous cliff down to the rich Kingside Mineral Vein. Successive rubble dams show how water was guided ever further south-west to wash topsoil and rock off the top of the lead- and silver-ore deposits below. RCAHMW

mine dressing floors as well as for workings underground.

Many of the larger concentrations of visible remains in the uplands today date from this period of large-scale production in the mid- and late nineteenth century. Some larger mines such as Frongoch and Cwmystwyth, both in the mining centre of upland north Ceredigion, could have at least fifteen waterwheels to drive the winding and pumping machinery at deep shafts. They also powered extensive washing and dressing machinery arranged on covered hillside terraces, with the increasingly concentrated ore being conveyed downhill to transportation points. Such sites often have the remains of large masonry wheel-pits, stone-revetted dressing terraces and thick-walled crusher houses at their summits. Webs of narrow linear terraces that once carried small mineral railways and a

larger number of water-power channels or 'leats' extend across the mine areas, with long water feeders extending to large, specially constructed water storage reservoirs on the uplands surrounding the mines.

The impact of mines on the landscape and economy of the uplands was in final decline by the second quarter of the twentieth century, but, even so, fifty-three mines (5 per cent) have been worked since 1920.

The mines extended high into the relatively inhospitable uplands, and the water powering the later mines often froze in the winter. Of all the non-ferrous metals mines above the 200-metre contour about half (47 per cent), a total of five hundred and sixteen mines, are to be found on the upland fringe (between the 200- and 250- metres contours). Another third,

Hafotty Mines, Barmouth: a long line of nineteenth-century manganese workings leading south across coastal uplands towards the mouth of the Mawddach Estuary. There are banks of spoil on the downhill side to the right and some prospecting trenches at right angles near the bottom and in the middle. 93-cs-1003

(opposite) *Big Pit, Blaenafon: aerial view of Big Pit, the National Mining Museum of Wales, set on the western side of the upper valley of the Afon Llwyd. The shaft of 1860 was sunk to earlier 1830s' iron-ore and coal workings supplying the Blaenafon Ironworks, and buildings were added until the colliery ceased coal production in 1980. The workers' baths and canteen building of 1939 in the foreground is in the International Modernist style universally used by the Miners' Welfare Committee. 99-cs-0352*

metres, the highest being the copper mine of Clogwyn Coch on the flanks of Snowdon, at approximately 770 metres in height!

Upland Iron, Coal and Slate in the Industrial Revolution

Some of the most important early industrial sites in the world are in the uplands of Wales; this has been recognised by the award of World Heritage status to the industrial landscape of Blaenafon. In the first half of the nineteenth century the largest ironworks on Earth in the world's first Industrial Revolution were built in the Heads of the Valleys area (*Blaenau*) of south-eastern Wales, where even the towns in the valley bottoms are at a height of over 244 metres.

The complex landscape that remains comprises much more than the stone-built furnaces of the works themselves. The works were built here because the necessary raw materials were available in the underlying geology: the north-eastern edge of the coalfield provided bituminous coal for coking and blackband iron-ores for feeding the furnaces. Limestone, found just to the north of the coal deposits, provided the necessary flux for the furnaces, and in the millstone grit in between were silica sand deposits that could be used in the production of fire-bricks for furnace linings. Quarries and mines were required to work all these.

In addition to these were many linear features linking the works and extractive points in the landscape, as well as watercourses (leats), which provided power to the works and mines. Since the Aberfan disaster of 1965 the land reclamation programme has removed many of these relict landscapes. The Uplands Initiative now targets the remaining areas, and the surveys done have demonstrated the considerable interest of the landscapes that remain.

Four areas have been surveyed that include the mineral extraction and waterpower generation fields of what were the three largest ironworks internationally in the first half of the nineteenth century: Cyfarthfa and Dowlais Ironworks at

three hundred and sixty-four mines, lie between 250 and 350 metres in height. There are only ten per cent, one hundred and fourteen mines, between the 350- and 450-metres contour, with only 5 per cent, fifty mines, above 450 metres, where conditions must have been arduous and difficult. Not surprisingly, only three or four of these sites lie above 690

49

Merthyr Tydfil (Tudful), and the Blaenafon Ironworks. Survey has revealed that the uplands above the ironworks are criss-crossed by the earthworks of large waterpower channels and reservoirs. The densest example was called the Dowlais Free Drainage System, and survey has revealed that there are the remains of thirty-eight reservoirs or water-storage ponds. These were interconnected by a web of leats which also operated the haulage in many colliery shafts, with filled water tanks attached to lift cages making many empty cages descend and propelling loaded cages upward; the watercourses also drove waterwheels in the ironworks. A detailed survey of this internationally significant industrial landscape was carried out

Grawen Early Railway Depot: this depot at 380 metres above sea-level in the western Brecon Beacons has left behind impressive earthwork remains. There were several depots servicing a network of early horse-worked railways that was one of the most developed transport infrastructures of the first three decades of the nineteenth century. The lines carried coal, limestone and iron-ore. The labour-force was housed in traditional earth-walled cottages with stone chimney-stacks, constructed by the local Brecon Forest Tramroad Company in the later 1820s. RCAHMW

Clydach terraces, Brynmawr: the uplands of the Heads of the Valleys area (the Blaenau) show rapidly disappearing examples of early-nineteenth-century shallow opencast workings on the northern fringe of the coalfield. Brynmawr is at top left, with the Heads of the Valleys Road at upper left and a twentieth-century water-supply reservoir below Beaufort at upper right. The crescent-shaped trench at left is the remains of early open workings along a five-feet coal seam with iron-ore workings to the right and a mixture of iron-ore and coal workings to the left. 92-cs-1066

by the Royal Commission prior to the intended implementation of a large scheme to opencast coal and then 'reclaim' the area.

Water was used for a variety of purposes in these upland landscapes. One was scouring, or hushing, whereby the topsoil was removed by the release of periodic rushes of water from fairly small embanked ponds. There are quite impressive examples of these, with the large gashes across the landscape produced by them, near Keeper's Pond at Blaenafon and on the upland common to the east of Blaenafon town (Hayman

and Horton 2001). Other good examples in the areas covered by Uplands Initiative surveys include Upper Race (i.e. a 'race' of water) above Pontypool (Bick 1994; GGAT 1997g) and the maze of water channels at Cwmystwyth lead mine in mid-Wales (Hughes 1994; Sambrook and Hankinson 2001).

Dense complexes of early horse-worked railways were also constructed to link multiple short-lived coal and iron-ore mines and limestone quarries to the ironworks and onto the nearest canal taking the ironworks' products to the coast and further afield. The long lengths of experimentally engineered

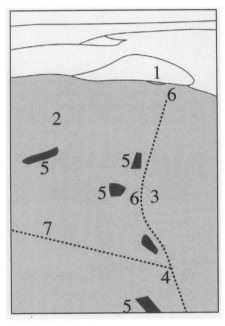

Hill's Pits, Blaenafon: the main upland coal-mining field to the north of Blaenafon Ironworks (1). Water-scouring and shallow mining tunnels are visible (2), with the large earthworks of World War II opencast workings above. Shafts of coal-mines visible include Hill's Pits of 1844 (3) and Balance and New Pit (4). In the early nineteenth century colliery lift cages ascending were balanced by filled water-tanks descending; the tanks were supplied from the ponds (5) and watercourses visible. The formation of a horse-drawn railway leading to the ironworks is visible (6) together with the Dyne-Steel railway inclined-plane of c.1850 (7). 99-cs-0374

Big Pit, Blaenafon: a ground view of Big Pit showing the random assemblage of buildings of various dates and characteristic of upland mine sites in Wales. C99006

and worked lines built in south Wales at the end of the eighteenth and beginning of the nineteenth centuries were a crucial stage in the development of the modern railway. The railways recorded in the upland landscape around Blaenafon have several features of international importance. What seems to have been the world's first high and multiple-arched railway viaduct was constructed at the same time as, or soon after, the opening of the Blaenafon Ironworks in 1788-9. It was constructed in order to allow coal and iron mines on the hillside to fuel the tops of the high iron furnaces via a level or slight downhill gradient, which eased the weight pulled by the horses operating the railway. The high arches also provided roofs for the dwellings of the first group of workers to reach these rather inhospitable uplands. Nineteenth-century writing makes it clear that soon after construction the viaduct was buried with waste from nearby limestone quarries. Examination of old maps has enabled the location of the viaduct to be re-established; excavation has re-exposed its deck (Hayman and Horton 2000, 2001; Blaenafon Aerial Mapping in NMRW; Timeteam excavation, 2000).

What was the longest railway tunnel in the world (Pwll-du: two kilometres long) is also located in the Blaenafon industrial landscape; the portals were recorded during the upland survey. Additional features relate to the horse-worked railways changing level: the tunnel was later replaced by a double ('Dyne-Steel') incline rising and then descending over the hill above, with a steam-engine for powering loaded trains placed on the summit. At Blaenafon there are also two impressive structures remaining where loaded wagons were raised by filled water tanks making empty lift-cages descend. One is the large 'water-balance' tower at the ironworks site itself and the other is the shaft and tunnel that allowed loaded limestone wagons to be raised from the Pwll-du Quarry.

One of the best examples of how a web of horse-worked railway tracks developed a mining field covering the outcropping of several successive seams of coal is shown by the Bryn-y-Gwyddel area of Merthyr Tydfil, which once formed part of the mining field of Cyfarthfa Ironworks – the world's largest in the first quarter of the nineteenth century (Frost and Jones 2000).

Slate-quarrying Landscapes

In the nineteenth century the north-western uplands of Wales became the home of the world's largest roofing-slate industry. Slate had been worked in Wales since Roman times, but the large-scale industry did not emerge until the eighteenth century (Gwyn 2000, 3). The largest quarries at Dinorwig (Llanberis) and Penrhyn (Bethesda) were opened at the end of the eighteenth century by aristocratic landowners amalgamating earlier small-scale workings. Other main centres of upland quarrying at Dyffryn Nantlle and Blaenau Ffestiniog were collections of many separate quarrying concerns. At its peak this largely upland industry employed fourteen thousand men and was still growing in the 1870s when it was a major supplier of roofing material to the burgeoning industrial towns and cities of Britain, mainland Europe and North America. The provision of employment on such a scale was culturally very important for supporting the continuance of a large Welsh-speaking population in the area. Scattered, self-built industrial communities spread across the hillsides of Moel Tryfan, Cilgwyn and at Deinolen for the huge Dinorwig Quarry. The now disused great working

Blaenau Ffestiniog: this still active slate-quarrying town is in the uplands; the survey area at Moel Bowydd is visible beyond. Oakeley Quarry (1818-) on the extreme left once employed some one thousand, seven hundred people producing sixty thousand tons of slate a year. Llechwedd Quarry (1846) at centre left has almost twenty miles of underground tunnels and extensive watercourses (leats) and reservoirs on the upland plateau beyond, while Bowydd/Diffwys Casson/Maenofferen (1760s-) Slate Quarries on the right have railway inclines leading up to and across the high upland. 96-cs-0728

terraces of the quarry still dominate the mountainside facing Snowdon itself.

The uplands of Snowdonia had many more smaller quarries, and like the upland industrial areas of the south they were linked by webs of horse-worked railways and water-channels fed from reservoirs, although such landscapes tend to be of the later, rather than the earlier, nineteenth century (Thompson 1998b). The railways of the industry extended through the mountains to the nearest ports, and their distinctive form spread throughout the developing upland areas of the world. The Penrhyn Quarry Railway of 1801 established a pattern that was adapted by the engineers of the Ffestiniog Railway for steam traction and passenger transport and was imitated by post-civil war railway developments in the USA, throughout the British Empire and in mainland Europe and Russia. The power requirements of the industry culminated in the construction of upland water reservoirs and pipelines to drive hydro-electric power stations at Cwm Croesor (1904), Pant yr Afon in Blaenau Ffestiniog (1904), Cwm Dyli (1906) and Maentwrog (1922) (Gwyn 2000, 8-9).

Industrial Workers in the Uplands

One of the distinctive features of the uplands is the intermittent ruined cottages and communities on the upland fringe, now often more obvious than the scant traces of some house-platforms and long-huts, but not always distinguishable from these earlier dwellings.

The widespread nature and large scale of upland mining and quarrying obviously had a significant impact on the character and balance of upland society. During the Uplands Initiative studies (Sambrook and Darke 1997, 23-6) have been made of the nature of settlement in north Ceredigion, where the densest concentration of upland non-ferrous mines in Wales existed.

The studies concern the uplands some sixteen to twenty-four kilometres east of Aberystwyth. In the uppermost reaches of Cwmrheidol, east of Ponterwyd, were the lead mines of Dyffryn Castell and Esgairlle. In this area the inhabitants of farmhouses very largely continued in traditional occupations, but occasionally the farmers' sons would be employed in the mines as these increased in scale and prosperity, particularly in the latter part of the nineteenth century. However, there was a far larger scale of change in the occupation of the many inhabitants of cottages in response to the varying opportunities of employment offered by the increasing prosperity of the lead mines. Cottages that had been empty or housed paupers, farm

Penarth Slate Quarry (1868-1932): the quarry terraces so typical of upland slate quarries rise through the centre of the picture, flanked by spoil tips of waste rock from each terrace. The ruins of dressing-sheds lie at the bottom of the quarry terraces and to the bottom left. Spoil heaps of waste rock from the dressing process lie at the bottom of the picture; they are bisected by a railway incline to convey the dressed slate away to market. 95-cs-0239

labourers or even a cooper in 1841 (1841 census) all housed lead-miners by 1881 (1881 census). On three sites the number of dwellings had doubled, with the new ones all occupied by lead-miners' families, and including a cottage added to a farmhouse. A lead-miner's house on a completely new site had also been built at Ty'n yr Ochr by 1881.

Bryngwyn Bach near Tregaron, Ceredigion. Irregular settlement pattern of a deserted 'squatter' community on upland common in an area of lead-mining and agricultural activity 2001-cs-0334

Cefnan near Bethesda, Gwynedd. Regular rows of 1870s cottages and gardens built on open upland by workers to designs by the Penrhyn Slate Quarry management. 99-cs-2054

The great lead mines near the head of the Ystwyth valley at Cwmystwyth were on a much larger scale and gave rise to a distinct settlement pattern of scattered miners' homesteads on land surrounded by rough open pasture. Like other typical '*tai-unnos*', or squatter settlements, these comprised cottages and houses loosely dispersed across poor-quality ground at high altitude at or beyond the margins of previous cultivation. A large settlement of this type occurs in the side valley of the Nant Gorlan to the north of the hamlet of Cwmystwyth and largely at altitudes between 300 and 450 metres. The still-occupied Cwm Gorlan settlement is visible from the Upland Trail recently established as part of the Mynydd y Ffynnon Project and has been researched for that purpose.

The size of the cottager community at Cwm Gorlan varied with the productivity of the Cwmystwyth Mine. In 1841 (1841 census) there were twenty-four households based on thirteen cottage sites. Each cottage site usually had one or two small fields and gardens enclosed from the upland waste. This upland cottage settlement had a population of one hundred and eleven in 1841, an average of about four and a half people per household. Eighty-eight per cent of households were led by people employed at the mine; only three out of twenty-four households were led by people on pensions or other independent means of income. None of the households were led by anybody in agricultural employment, although the subsidiary agricultural employment of the population on their own small gardens and fields did occur from time to time. Of the forty-one people employed at the mine (an average of 1.7 people per household) twenty-four were described as 'lead miners'– usually the male head of a household or older sons (although one female was so described). Fourteen 'wash miners' were made up of the women and children of the households, who were employed on the above-ground washing and dressing of the lead-ore. The only specialist craftsman was a blacksmith (there was a smithy at the mine), and two other inhabitants were labourers, almost certainly employed at the mine.

Twenty years later, in 1861 (1861 census), sixteen of the twenty occupation sites (80 per cent) had single occupancy, whereas ten years previously this proportion had been 60 per cent (nine households), and twenty years previously a mere 30 per cent (three households). The general move to roomier and better food-based sites involved the use of one new site and two that had previously been occupied but then abandoned. Against this trend was the building of four new dwellings on a single site (the appropriately named 'Tai Newyddion' or 'New Houses') and rebuilding on two occupation sites that had been abandoned since 1851. There was obviously a tendency to fluidity in the form of the settlement arising from the cheap and basic construction used.

The great Cwmystwyth Mine achieved its all-time productive peak in 1864 with one thousand, six hundred tons of lead-ore produced, and the increased employment prospects were reflected in a dramatic rise in the number employed in the mine (by 37 per cent) to seventy-two and an increase in the community's population by 65 per cent to one hundred and ninety-five by 1871 (1871 census). The number of households recorded had almost doubled at forty-two, but the number of sites occupied was little changed at twenty-two. The number of single-household sites almost halved from 80 per cent to 45 per cent (ten out of twenty-two sites). The economic maturity of the settlement showed in the fact that a tailor, an artisan whose occupation was unrelated to the mine, was the head of one of the households. Two daughters of households were dressmakers and one son was a postman. There were also a cooper and carrier whose trades were almost certainly related to the mine. However, the agricultural base underpinning the community showed through in the census entries for Thomas Thomas, the head of one of the households, who was recorded as a 'labourer and farmer', and the brother of another head of

household, who was identified as a farm labourer. However, employment in the lead mine still dominated the settlement, with forty-seven male lead miners and four labourers in the mines. Women and children made up the eighteen employed dressing and washing the lead-ore.

The mine and its dependent mining community were in rapid decline by the early 1890s. Lead-ore production (one hundred and fifty-three tons) was less than a tenth of the 1864 peak, although one hundred and twenty-eight tons of zinc blende were also produced. The population of the settlement dropped to one hundred and thirty-five by 1891 (1891 census), 69 per cent of its recorded peak of twenty years previously. Only twenty-three of the thirty-eight households (63%) were now dependent on the lead mine for income, and the drift to the booming, largely lowland coal mines of south Wales had started, with the coal-miner son of one of the lead-mining families being noted as being in residence at the time of the 1891 census. Five cottages were noted as being uninhabited in

Pentre-briwnant, Cwmystwyth: two typical upland miners' cottages on the roadside leading to Cwm Gorlan. 034_NC.jpg

Cwm Gorlan: this dispersed cottage group at Tai Newyddion, Cwmystwyth, was part of a lead miners' settlement which was in existence by the early nineteenth century. The first houses may have been tai unnos built on common land by squatters during the eighteenth century. 99-cs-0256

1891, and there is evidence that the inhabitants were diversifying their incomes.

The mine closed completely in 1893 and was only re-opened intermittently and on a small-scale between 1900 and final closure in the 1930s (Hughes, S. J. 1981, 33-45). The upland cottage community at Cwm Gorlan declined, but several of the cottage sites and their fields enclosed from the upland waste survive.

Cwm Gorlan is typical of many hundreds of such cottage communities that were established on the upland fringe, dependent both on mining and agriculture for their existence. Shepherds, hill-farmers, miners and peat-cutters all lived in these types of upland settlement. In historical terms the value of such evidence is that it shows how many upland cottages were abandoned, built and sometimes re-occupied during a relatively short space of years late in the nineteenth century. The apparently primitive nature of the many ruins of dwellings in Cwm Gorlan and elsewhere does not, despite appearances, necessarily indicate great antiquity.

The type of simple, self-built cottage constructed in these communities may have had much older antecedents in the abodes of the impoverished peasantry of the mid-Wales upland district (Sambrook 1995, 29). Many of the dwellings built on the marginal land of Ceredigion in the eighteenth and

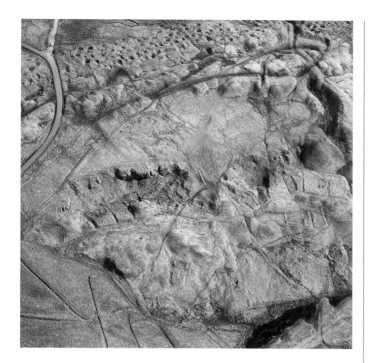

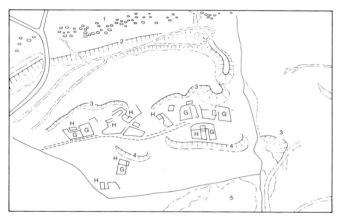

Shaft mounds – remains of old ironstone pits 2. Spoil tips from pit workings 3. Ironstone quarries 4. Spoil tips 5. Reclaimed area H. House G. Garden plot

'It was partly formed by an excavation in the slate rock, and partly by walls of mud mixed with chopped rushes, covered with segs, and having a wattled or basket work chimney. The entrance was in the gable end, facing the south east, which was defended during the night, or in very cold weather, by a wattled hurdle, clothed with rushes. A wall of turfs for fuel served as a partition for the bed-room, furnished with a bed of heath and dried rushes in one corner. The furniture was such as necessity dictated: some loose stones formed the grate; two large ones, with a plank across, supplied the place of chairs; a kettle, with a back stone for baking oaten cakes, answered every culinary purpose; and two coarse earthen pitchers stood by for the preserving or carrying water and dodgriafel, the usual beverage of the family…'

Many have left only ruins as mining and agricultural employment have declined. These types of ruins are an extremely widespread class of remains. Industrial landscape studies (Hayman and Horton 2000 and 2001; Hughes, S. R., 2000) have shown how the construction of on-site cottages and groups of houses accompanied the use of isolated mines and industrial installations: dwellings for key workers were constructed by iron- and copper-smelting companies operating their own mines, while other workers often constructed their own cottages. The upland survey of East Merthyr (Percival 1995) revealed a complete settlement constructed by quarry workers in piecemeal fashion on waste tips owned by the Penydarren Iron Company. In the uplands surrounding the largest slate quarries in north-west Wales, and those surrounding what were then the world's largest ironworks at the heads of the valleys of south-east Wales, quarry and works operators built much more ambitiously planned layouts of workers' housing. In the latter case these have evolved into, or form parts of, such present upland towns as Tredegar, Blaenafon and Merthyr Tydfil (Tudful).

nineteenth centuries were of this type, and the early, upland, horse-railway workers' cottages built in south-western Powys (Breconshire) in *c.*1828 (Hughes, S. R.1990, 205-07, 240-3) also continued this tradition in the southern uplands of Wales. The type was clearly described by the Reverend J. Evans in 1804 (Evans 1804, 349), when, having entered a peat-cutter's home at Ystrad Meurig in the northern Ceredigion uplands, the home of a family of two adults and three children, he noted:

Garnddyrys Forge: the dark green area below the turnpike road is the dry bed of one of the large ponds that stored water for powering the works (1817-c.1864). Below that is a square area of smooth turf that was surrounded by workers' houses on three sides. To the right of the pond is a hollow that was the cellar of the manager's house, and to its left are the foundations of iron rolling-mills that were driven by a large waterwheel. Just below the stone boundary wall running diagonally across the picture from bottom left is an early horse-worked railway tunnel under the works' tips. 94-cs-0621

CASE STUDIES

THE BLAENAFON UPLANDS LANDSCAPE

Richard Hayman and Wendy Horton (Hayman & Horton)

One of the best-preserved industrial landscapes in Wales and now a designated World Heritage Site, Blaenafon lies at the north-east corner of the South Wales Coalfield. In a classic valleys setting, Blaenafon town is near the head of the Afon Llwyd, sheltered by Coity Mountain to the south-west and the Blorenge to the north-east, rising to 581 and 552 metres respectively, while on the north side of the town is a plateau known as Pwll-du, beyond which the terrain falls to the Usk valley further north.

Before the present Uplands Initiative was begun there had been several surveys of the Blaenafon landscape, but none of them was exhaustive or covered the entire geographical area (e.g. Parry 1964; van Laun 1979; Lowe and Lawlor 1980). The primary purpose of the present survey was, therefore, to provide a comprehensive record of upland sites. In the process it was also intended to stimulate new approaches to its

interpretation and to provide a fuller understanding of its historic importance. The latter is a key element in drawing up a plan for the long-term management of the archaeological resource. The Blaenafon landscape was tolerably well understood before the start of the survey, and recognition of its importance is of course implicit in World Heritage Site status. However, that does not mean that its history is in any way fully understood.

The key elements of its history are well known and are based on the extraction of coal, iron ore (ironstone) and limestone, which are the raw materials used in the smelting of iron. Previously the landscape had been primarily given over to sheep grazing, with enclosed land and scattered farmsteads confined to the sheltered valley floors, as can still be seen in Cwm Llanwenarth on the north side of Pwll-du. Small-scale working of coal and ironstone had started by the late

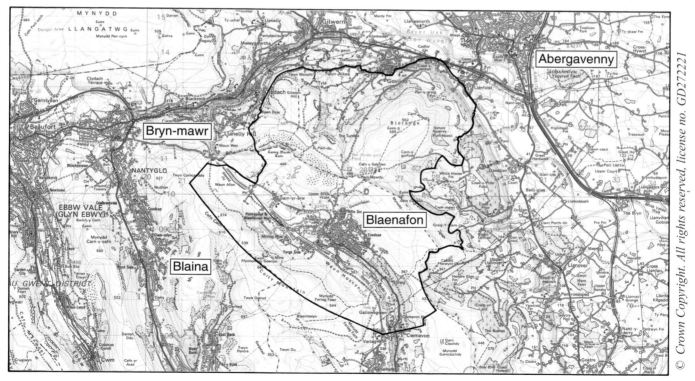

The Blaenafon uplands survey area, defining the area of survey in 1992 onwards.

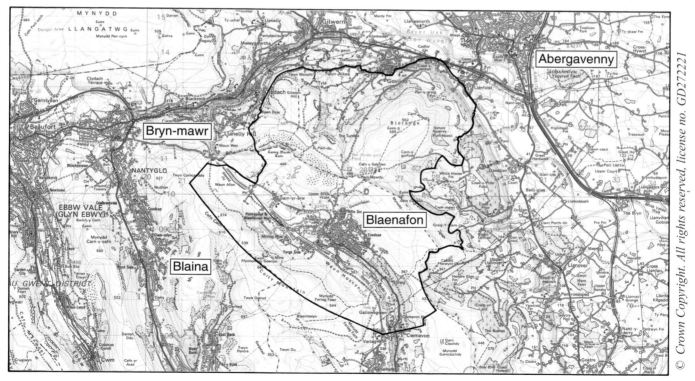

The Blaenafon uplands survey area, defining the area of survey in 1992 onwards.

61

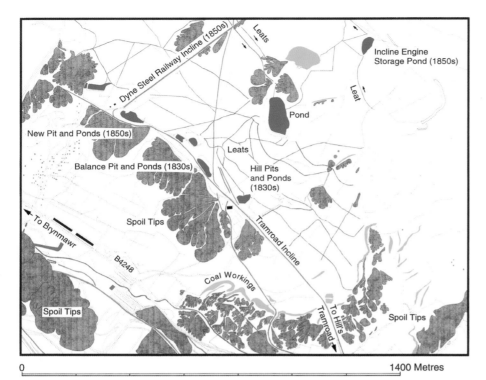

Air photo mapping of coal workings and a multitude of other features around Hill's Pits, Blaenafon, compiled from vertical and oblique aerial photographs, and historic maps and surveys. The detailed overall mapping of the Blaenafon World Heritage Site by RCAHMW, of which this is a part, revealed for the first time its complexity. It provides a detailed base map against which new field recording programmes within the Uplands Initiative, and new management schemes, can be planned. RCAHMW.

seventeenth century. Large-scale industrial development began when Lord Abergavenny leased the mineral rights in 1788 to a partnership of businessmen resident in the English Midlands – Thomas Hill, Benjamin Pratt and Thomas Hopkin (originally from Wales) – who founded the Blaenafon Ironworks (Knight 1989). The area of the lease corresponds roughly with the area encompassed by the World Heritage Site.

Mineral exploitation at Blaenafon followed a general pattern seen elsewhere in the 'Heads of the Valleys' ironworking district. At first coal and ironstone were both exploited, beginning with the most easily accessible deposits. Subsequently coal-mining increased as the quantity of iron smelted also increased, but the exploitation of iron ore declined as the ironworks relied upon cheaper or higher quality imports. By the mid-nineteenth century mining of iron had ceased, but the collieries expanded because there was a growing market for coal as a product in its own right.

Movement of raw materials required a complex transport infrastructure, principally consisting of iron plateways, known in the district as tramroads. Originally the finished iron was sent southward to the head of the Monmouthshire Canal at Pontypool (Pont-y-pwl). The Brecknock & Abergavenny Canal was built in 1797-1800 and passes on the north side of

Blaenafon, but it could not be fully exploited by the ironmasters until a tramroad was built in 1817 to link it with Blaenafon. Known as Hill's Tramroad, it incorporated a tunnel over a mile in length and inclines to negotiate the steep descent to canal level. At the same time the company built a forge at Garnddyrys beside the tramroad in an otherwise isolated location. The canal was superseded after the Monmouthshire Railway & Canal Company opened its branch railway line to Blaenafon in 1854. This prompted the closure of Garnddyrys, and its replacement by a new plant at Blaenafon known as Forge Side, where blast furnaces were also built, the first of which was blown-in in 1868. Throughout this period limestone was quarried to be used as a flux in the blast furnaces. Quarrying continued after smelting ceased at Blaenafon in 1913.

The iron industry gradually altered the character of the landscape, which changed again in the latter half of the twentieth century as the coal industry declined. The last phase of coal-mining in the mid-twentieth century included large opencast workings that destroyed some of the earlier evidence of coal and ironstone working. Elsewhere derelict sites such as the old Forge Side works and colliery sites near the town, like the Kay and Garn drift mines that continued working to the 1960s, were subject to land reclamation. Nevertheless the

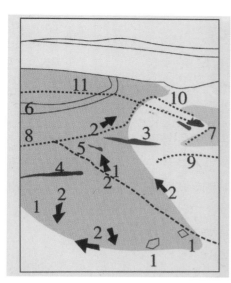

Pen-ffordd-goch, Blaenafon: view from the north-eastern upland edge of the South Wales Coalfield (shaded brown). Scouring (hushing) with water from short-lived ponds (1) and watercourses took place from the seventeenth century, although most of the substantial deep gullies produced are known to have been used in the early nineteenth century (2). Scouring on the north had stopped by 1817 when the upper reservoir (3 – Keeper's / Forge Pond Pen-ffordd-goch) for powering Garnddyrys Forge was constructed. Mining tunnels (adits) were driven into the sides of deeply scoured gullies (4) by 1812. Spoil mounds from early shallow mine-shafts (5) are visible, as are large opencast trenches (6) made in World War II to dig out shallow coal seams. By Pwll-du Limestone Quarry (7) can be seen the cart-road that carried limestone (shaded green) to the Blaenafon Ironworks from 1789. The formation of the first horse-drawn railway (1796) that took limestone from quarries on Blorenge Mountain to the ironworks can also be seen. The formation of Hill's Tramroad of 1817 is visible leading to the ironworks through the Pwll-du Tunnel, as is the line of its successor – the Dyne-Steel Railway Inclined-plane of c.1850 – over the top of the mountain. 99-cs-0368

Hill's Tramroad: terraced loop of the upland horse-worked railway that formerly connected Blaenafon Ironworks to the Brecknock & Abergavenny Canal. The ruined building alongside the railway formation at centre right was formerly a smithy and house in which a school for the Garnddyrys Works children was also held. C99007

majority of the relict historic landscape is especially well preserved. The original Blaenafon Ironworks escaped demolition and in 1975 became a guardianship monument in the care of Cadw. The last working colliery in the district, Big Pit, became an independent museum after its closure in 1980, and is now part of the National Museums & Galleries of Wales.

Fieldwork at Blaenafon was preceded by a programme of historic map digitisation and air photograph mapping, undertaken by RCAHMW. This involved the scanning of mid-twentieth-century vertical air photographs and their incorporation into a digital version of Ordnance Survey mapping using GIS software. Likewise early large-scale Ordnance Survey maps, beginning with the first edition in 1880-1 and also using the revised editions of 1901 and 1922, were incorporated in digital form, supplemented by information from surveys of the locality in 1812, 1814 and 1829. The result was the production of a map of the survey area describing the likely location and extent of sites on the ground.

The digitisation of map and photographic information

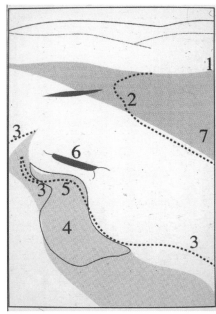

Pwll-du Limestone Quarries, Blaenafon: the lip of the north-eastern edge of the South Wales Coalfield (shaded brown) with its bordering narrow outcrops of upland millstone grit and limestone (shaded green) forms the upland bluff towering above Abergavenny (Y Fenni). At first the limestone was transported to Blaenafon Ironworks (1) across the mountain (2), but by 1817 a horse-drawn railway (Hill's Tramroad (3)) through Pwll-du Tunnel connected the two. The limestone produced at Pwll-du Quarry, sited right on the edge of the uplands, was taken up to the railway via a water-balance lift powered by water from the reservoir (6) above. Iron ore and coal (7) were water-scoured nearby from shallow deposits on the edge of the coalfield. The water pond towards the top of the picture (Keeper's Pond or Pond Pen-ffordd-goch) provided power for driving the rolling-mills at the nearby Garnddyrys Forge of 1817. 99-cs-0385

Pen-ffordd-goch, Blaenafon: a deep hushed gully produced by scouring with successive rushes of water from a small reservoir in order to expose and work seams of iron-ore and coal. Seventeenth to early nineteenth century in date. C99002

cannot be used as a substitute for field survey. As a collation of previous surveys it cannot claim to be a record of what still exists and does not claim to capture every site. Aerial photography, for example, is limited by what is visible in specific lighting and seasonal conditions. In fact fieldwork showed that the GIS project captured the vast majority but not all of the sites that survived. It also documented losses of sites due to later opencast working and land reclamation, which by their nature erase the historic landscape.

It is important to understand that aerial mapping can describe archaeological features but it cannot interpret them. Interpretation is therefore the other primary objective of the survey. Fieldwork was conducted by walking in parallel 30-metre transects to find and record archaeological features.

Despite being a mechanical process field-walking is an exercise in developing interpretation. The survey of a comparatively recent landscape also brought into focus the problems of drawing a boundary between what is and what is not archaeology. The large mid-twentieth-century opencast is a site in its own right and a late phase in a long sequence of coal-mining. However, if it is regarded as archaeology then so must be earlier twentieth-century sites such as a pair of radio transmission masts, and likewise the butts of nineteenth-century rifle ranges. By contrast numerous late-nineteenth-century houses that have been effectively reinvented by modernisation were not included on the database.

How is the Blaenafon survey changing our interpretation of the landscape? As occurred in association with other upland extractive industries, settlements were established that have subsequently disappeared. This is evident at Pwll-du on the north side of Blaenafon, where an isolated settlement, large enough to include a chapel, vanished when quarrying ceased. Previous studies of workmen's housing in the South Wales valleys have focused on the preference for building in rows (Lowe 1985). However, at Pwll-du, although such housing existed, dwellings were often individual or pairs of cottages situated close to the place of work or conveniently adjacent to the main tramroads. These cottages were always provided with walled enclosures that were large enough to accommodate grazing of livestock as well as vegetable plots, many of which survive. The presence of individual cottages on the exposed common land does not conform to the pattern of post-medieval farmsteads that is visible in the lower, more sheltered areas. It raises the probability that workmen employed in the extractive industries of Blaenafon were engaged in both industry and farming, as was the case in the upland slate and lead-mining industries.

The other important issue that the survey has highlighted is the significance of the time-scale at Blaenafon, where changes in extractive methods are discernible from the eighteenth to the mid-twentieth centuries. The ironstone workings are generally early – between 1790 and 1830. Ironstone was worked from the surface in a process known as patching, but where the ironstone beds lay below the surface the overburden had first to be cleared away. This was achieved by storing and then releasing a torrent of water to wash the surface material away, a technique known here as scouring. These workings, often linear in form because a particular vein has been followed, remain conspicuous features, not least because ironstone working produced large tips of shale waste. The more subtle features associated with these surface workings are levels driven from them, which cannot be detected using aerial mapping. Underground ironstone workings have left few surface traces, and consequently the mining landscape north of the town retains an early-nineteenth-century character.

At Blaenafon evidence of eighteenth-century coal-workings, in the form of bell pits, has been buried by the encroaching opencast tips. One of the characteristics of the early-nineteenth-century collieries of South Wales was the use of water-balance lifts, whereby the weight of water counterbalanced the weight of coal at the bottom of the shaft. Cheap and effective, water-balance lifts were used in shallow, self-draining pits. In the Blaenafon landscape there is evidence of three pits where water-balance lifts were used. Hill's Pit, Balance Pit and New Pit were all sunk between 1835 and 1848 on the north-west side of Blaenafon. They have an interconnecting network of leats feeding a line of reservoirs close to the former pits, which collected the other major resource of the Welsh hills – rainwater. Two other sites in the district also retain evidence of water-balance lifts for raising and lowering materials at different surface-levels. One is a rare surviving lift built in 1839 at the ironworks itself. Another comprises leat, pond and lift shaft at the Pwll-du limestone quarry. The final main technological development extant in the area is steam-powered winding of deep mines, and is represented at Big Pit where in 1952, as in other contemporary collieries, the original steam-engine was replaced by an electric winder (Thomas 1981). The other evidence of these later workings is subsidence associated with late-nineteenth-century drift mines. In the form of steep-sided pits, they are superficially similar to naturally occurring pits where limestone outcrops.

Limestone quarrying can also be studied chronologically, from the small-scale workings on the north side of the Blorenge to the late-nineteenth-century quarry at Cefn-y-lan, each with its own tramroad. At the Tyla Quarries, on the north-west side of the survey area, is an extensive quarry with late-nineteenth- and twentieth-century features such as limekilns and railway sidings. Together they demonstrate the increasing scale of limestone quarrying from the eighteenth to the early-twentieth centuries.

The extensive survey has, by giving equal weight to remains of all periods, highlighted the significance of the later sites in addition to the already well-documented earlier sites. It has also highlighted the potential for improving our understanding of upland settlement. These issues must be incorporated into the interpretation and management of the Blaenafon landscape to ensure that they receive adequate protection.

MYNYDD Y FFYNNON: CWMYSTWYTH AND EISTEDDFA GURIG

Paul Sambrook (Cambria Archaeology)

Introduction

The Mynydd y Ffynnon Archaeological Survey was initiated by Forest Enterprise and the Royal Commission and undertaken jointly by Cambria Archaeology (the Dyfed Archaeological Trust) and the Clwyd-Powys Archaeological Trust between 1996 and 2001. It was funded, with EU assistance, by ADAS, Forest Enterprise and the Royal Commission.

The Mynydd y Ffynnon study extended across one hundred square kilometres of mostly upland landscape in the Cambrian Mountains, straddling the historic border between north-eastern Ceredigion and Powys. The area was defined by four river valleys, namely those of the Ystwyth to the south,

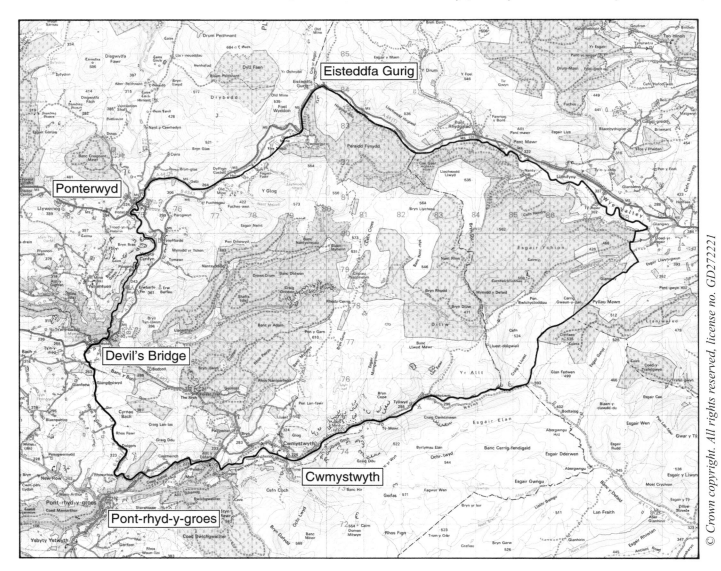

The Mynydd y Ffynnon project area in north Ceredigion.

the Rheidol to the west, the Castell to the north and the Wye (and its Tarenig tributary) to the east.

Within the study area large tracts of land are blanketed by coniferous plantations owned by Forest Enterprise. ADAS has an extensive holding focused on its farm at Pwllpeiran. Privately-owned farms also account for a large proportion of the locality, particularly along the river valleys which border each side of it.

Project Methodology

A survey of such a large area over such an extended time period posed both a challenge and an opportunity. From the outset an element of desktop research was considered vital to complement the fieldwork component. This included consulting historic documents and maps held at the National Library of Wales, Aberystwyth, as well as the analysis of aerial photographs of the area, held by the Royal Commission.

Fieldwork succeeded in covering all unforested land within the survey area. This included a wide range of environments, from fertile pasture fields in the valley floors to exposed, rugged peat moorland on the open mountain tops. Within the afforested land all known sites identified by previous fieldwork or from aerial photographs and historic maps were visited. In some afforested areas prospecting was carried out to locate new archaeological sites, with some important successes. Field visits offered valuable opportunities to discuss aspects of landscape and social history with local people, and, where possible, oral testimony was collected to help inform the archaeological record.

The details of all recorded sites were entered in the regional Sites and Monuments Records (SMRs) held by Cambria Archaeology and the Clwyd-Powys Archaeological Trust. This information has been fed into the National Monuments Record of Wales (NMRW) held by the Royal Commission in Aberystwyth.

The results of the project have allowed the development of an outline of the history of the Mynydd y Ffynnon area over a period of some 4,000 years. However, it is important to emphasise that the Mynydd y Ffynnon Project, in common with many archaeological projects undertaken by the Welsh Archaeological Trusts, was necessarily about recording and managing evidence of the past, not researching and interpreting that evidence in detail. The issues surrounding the management of the archaeological resource are addressed elsewhere in this monograph.

Prehistory

The Mynydd y Ffynnon area is a landscape rich in prehistoric archaeology relating mostly to funerary monuments, but including possible evidence of early metal mining. There is little trace of human activity in the locality before the Bronze Age, but an unfinished stone mace-head of possibly Mesolithic date has been found near Cwmystwyth.

Cwmystwyth Lead-mine: the impact of centuries of mining activity at Cwmystwyth has left a scarred, yet dramatic and beautiful, landscape, rich in archaeological content. 95-cs-0418

It is thought likely that early prehistoric human communities located in the area which now lies under the waters of Cardigan Bay and along the modern coastal strip may have exploited the Ceredigion uplands as seasonal hunting grounds. As sea levels rose gradually after the Ice Age human

Cae Gaer Roman Fortlet, Llangurig: sited on a remote natural terrace overlooking the pass between the Tarenig and Castell valleys. This pass is an historic communications route linking east and west Wales, and which must have been of strategic importance to the Romans. 2001-cs-0389

they were located in the shelter of the valley. Future work may uncover more information about what must have been a regionally important focus of Bronze Age settlement, industry and trade.

Throughout the Iron Age, Roman and Early Medieval periods the hills of the region may have been exploited by pastoral farmers, but there is no evidence of settlement dating to these periods. Metal mining may have continued in the area, but there is currently no direct evidence for this either. A small Roman fortlet at Cae Gaer, Llangurig, is the only known site of Roman date in the area. The fortlet is positioned on a terrace overlooking the watershed between the Castell and Tarenig valleys, a pass through the hills which was probably a well-used communication route in the late Iron Age and Roman period. An unusual rectilinear earthwork in the Castell valley, known as 'Llys Arthur', may be a defensive structure guarding the same path, but, despite its evocative name, there is no evidence to indicate its true function or date.

Saints and Monks

One glimmer of light that may be thrown on the Early Medieval period is a possible Early Christian focus at Llaneithyr, near Devils Bridge, recorded for the first time by the project. Llaneithyr is an abandoned farmstead, but its name is that of a church dedicated to a Celtic saint – Eithyr being a personal name. Two fields near the farm are named by

Nant y Gafod: farmhouse ruins viewed from the south. Nant y Gafod is mentioned in early-sixteenth-century rent rolls of Strata Florida Abbey (Abaty Ystrad Fflur) as a possession of the abbey being rented to lay tenants. The farm was abandoned in the later nineteenth century. 1048-18

activity must have been pushed further eastwards, but little can be said about when and why the first human communities settled permanently in the Mynydd y Ffynnon area.

The first real evidence of such settlement is provided by the concentration of Bronze Age funerary cairns along the margins of the upper Ystwyth valley. Prior to the Mynydd y Ffynnon survey a few cairns were known north and south of the Ystwyth, along with a 3-metre high standing stone of possible Bronze Age date at Ysbyty Cynfyn church.

One of the major successes of the project was to increase the number of recorded Bronze Age funerary monuments within the survey area. Most of these new discoveries were made in the Ystwyth valley. This concentration of Bronze Age monuments is made all the more interesting by the proximity of the metal mines at Copa Hill, Cwmystwyth, which have provided radiocarbon dates that may indicate that copper was being mined here as early as 1800BC; antler picks of prehistoric date have also been found (Timberlake and Mighall 1992). The evidence suggests that Bronze Age communities were settled in the upper Ystwyth valley, but we cannot yet identify the locations of the settlements. Possibly

the parish tithe survey (Llanfihangel y Creuddyn Tithe Map) as *Cae Ffynnon Saint* (Saint's Well Field) and *Mynwent Fach* (Little Cemetery), apparently confirming that a lost ecclesiastical site lies here. *Mynwent Fach* was originally a small circular field and may be an Early Medieval *llan* site.

It is not until later-medieval and early post-medieval times that a clearer picture of settlement and landscape management comes into focus. This is in association with the history of the

Pant yr Allor, Tyllwyd Farm, Cwmystwyth: 'The Hollow of the Altar' is the site of three large building platforms, the largest of which can be seen in the centre of this photograph, with a person standing at its farthest edge. The name may indicate that a medieval grange chapel was once found here. This site is also suspected to be associated with the lost "Hafod y Adad", a medieval hafod in the possession of the abbot of Strata Florida (Ystrad Fflur). 13062-16

Lluest at Dolygors: a 'lluest' - type deserted settlement at Dolygors Farm, near Devils Bridge (Pontarfynach). The long-hut in the centre of the photograph is associated with a cultivated area visible just above it. CS. MF2

Cwmystwyth Grange of the Cistercian Abbey of Strata Florida, Ceredigion (Williams 1965). Founded by the Lord Rhys in 1164, Strata Florida was gifted substantial granges within Ceredigion and had rights of common pasture across the whole of the region's uplands, with much emphasis put on pastoral farming. In 1212 the abbey was granted a special license to export wool by King John, emphasising the importance of sheep to the abbey's estates.

The Cwmystwyth Grange undoubtedly specialised in sheep rearing, a farming tradition maintained unbroken to the present day. One local saying, "a man raised on sheep's milk is twice the man as one raised on cows' milk," is clearly deeply rooted in the farming community and serves to remind us that dairying in these hills in the past was as much to do with milking sheep as with milking cows.

The archaeological expression of this tradition is represented by a great number of long-huts and abandoned upland farmsteads dotted across the whole survey area and once occupied by shepherds and pastoral farmers. This is by no means an unspoilt wilderness – the landscape has been settled, managed and farmed for many centuries, no more so than under the management of the monks of Strata Florida, for whom wool and food were produced in surplus for sale and export. The Cwmystwyth Grange's pastoral character can be seen in its division into four *hafod* units in medieval times (areas of summer pasturage): Hafod Uchtryd; Hafod Uchared; Hafod Gau; Hafod yr Abad (Morgan 1991). The possible site of the latter was found by project staff in 2001 on a sheltered terrace high up on the northern side of the Ystwyth valley (Sambrook 2001). The complex includes several long-huts and ancillary features, including a unusually large 'sunken shelter' (probably a subterranean cool-store for dairy produce). This *hafod*, like many others, developed into a permanent upland farmstead and survived into post-medieval times.

For at least five hundred years the local landscape has been characterised by open mountain pastures, with arable farming only possible in the floors of the main valleys and some sheltered tributary valleys. The bare hills were described as such by John Leland when he passed through the area in 1526 (Hearne 1745). Surviving early-sixteenth-century rent rolls from Strata Florida (Morgan 1991) show that by that time there were many well established farms in the area being rented by the abbey to lay-farmers. The names of farmsteads such as Dolwen, Tygwyn, Blaen Myherin, Nant y Gafod, Hafod yr Abad, Dolygors, Cae'r Meirch, Hafod Uchtryd, Pwllpeiran, Bwlch yr Oerfa and Brignant appear in these lists, many of which are now deserted.

The Landscape Movement: Thomas Johnes of Hafod

With the Dissolution of the monasteries Strata Florida's granges passed into private hands, with much of the land of Cwmystwyth Grange being transferred to what became the Hafod estate, focused on Hafod Uchtryd, near Cwmystwyth (Kerkham and Briggs 1991). The Johnes family had possession by the mid-eighteenth century. Thomas Johnes, the family's most famous son, came into his inheritance in 1783 and immediately set about transforming the estate. Construction of the house in a gothic style commenced in the mid-1780s, and most of the garden features and picturesque landscape elements were in place by the time that George Cumberland published his description of Hafod in 1796: a

kitchen garden with long conservatory, a walled flower garden, long walks, a cold bath, summerhouses, lodges, drives and bridges. Hafod became celebrated: no tour of Wales was complete without a visit to the wonders of Johnes's creation (Kerkham 1991). Descriptions were written in diaries, journals and books, artists painted scenes, and views were even reproduced on a dinner service.

Demolition of the mansion was finalised in 1958, and many of the picturesque landscape features have disappeared under coniferous forestry plantations. Fieldwork and documentary research by interested individuals and organisations have revealed much that was considered lost. Archaeological work commissioned by Hafod Trust and Forest Enterprise since 1991 as part of a restoration process includes the compilation of a GIS archaeological database, small-scale excavation such as that carried out on the courses of the walks and cold bath, and topographic survey across large tracts of the landscape (Murphy nd.).

Johnes was also an agricultural improver and he established an experimental farm at Pwllpeiran, where he endeavoured to grow crops and plants (including yams) that might flourish in this rugged upland area (Linnard 1982, 108-20). It is possible that a series of unusual raised beds in the garden enclosures of the deserted Bwlch yr Oerfa farmstead (Briggs 1991b; a Scheduled Ancient Monument), which is adjacent to Pwllpeiran, are evidence of some of Johnes's agricultural experiments.

Brignant Isaf Farm: ruins near Devils Bridge (Pontarfynach). Brignant was a property of Strata Florida Abbey (Abaty Ystrad Fflur) in medieval times and was occupied into the twentieth century. 35313-24

Metal Mining

Metal mining has left a huge impact on the landscape of the Mynydd y Ffynnon area. When Lewis Morris re-opened the Nantycreiau Mine in the mid-eighteenth century he described old 'Roman' workings at the site. Such old workings may have been medieval, or Roman, or indeed prehistoric; we cannot know for certain, but it is evident that there was a mining tradition well established before the Industrial Revolution. In 1526 John Leland explained away the bareness of the local mountains as the result of tree-felling to provide fuel to lead smelteries in Cwmystwyth, an indication of the scale of mining there when the area was under the control of Strata Florida Abbey.

The Industrial Revolution saw an expansion of mining activity. Ruined buildings, shafts, levels and spoil tips at mines such as Nantycreiau, Tygwyn, Crown, Castell, Esgairlle, Nanty, Brignant, as well as the huge operation at Cwmystwyth, are lasting reminders of the industrial endeavours of the nineteenth century. Mining-related archaeology is not confined

RECONSTRUCTION OF AGRICULTURAL SETTLEMENT ON BWLCH-YR-OERFA

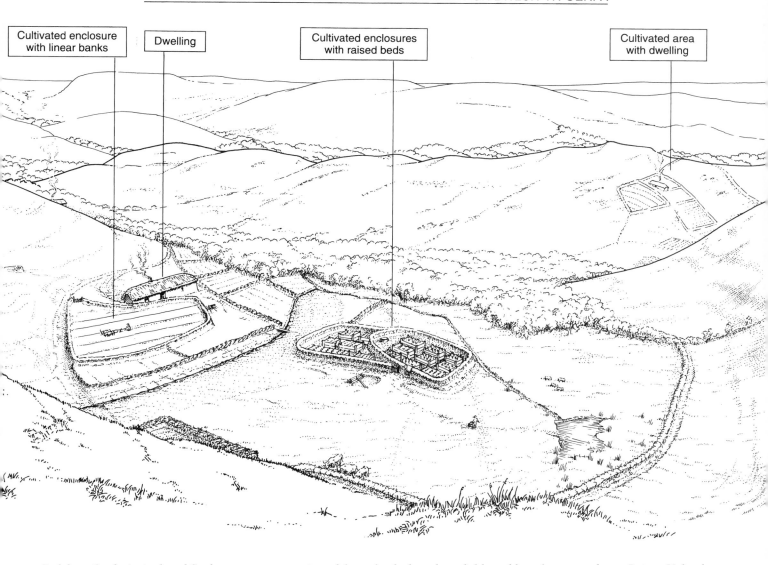

Cultivated enclosure with linear banks

Dwelling

Cultivated enclosures with raised beds

Cultivated area with dwelling

Bwlch-yr-Oerfa Agricultural Settlement: reconstruction of the embanked gardens, fields and long-hut as used on a Peiran Upland Trail Interpretation Board. RCAHMW drawing

Hafodydd at Tyllwyd: an unnamed deserted settlement high above Tyllwyd Farm, Cwmystwyth (seen in valley bottom). Human habitation reached on to the higher ground in this area during medieval and early post-medieval times. Sites such as this may have begun as seasonal hafodydd and developed into permanent settlements by the seventeenth or eighteenth centuries; those on higher ground were usually abandoned before the nineteenth century. 13062-34

to the mines themselves. Across the wider landscape there are also extensive leat systems and reservoirs that were built to supply sufficient water to power the machinery needed to raise and process the ore. The industrial expansion also impacted greatly on the settlement pattern of the area, with the increased population building new homes. This is mostly clearly seen at Cwmystwyth village and Tai Newyddion, where many miners' cottages still stand. This burst of industrial activity fell away quickly in the late-nineteenth century when metal ore prices fell sharply on the world market. The local mines closed and the population rapidly declined.

Conclusion

The Mynydd y Ffynnon survey has shown that this largely uninhabited landscape, large parts of which are now obscured by coniferous forest plantations, has a tremendous wealth of archaeological and historical evidence. It is in many ways a landscape filled with the 'ghosts' of the past. Through careful recording, protection and promotion its heritage can become a major new asset which may serve the communities of the area as they seek to sustain themselves during the twenty-first century.

MOEL BRONYMIOD

Katherine Geary (Gwynedd Archaeological Trust)

Introduction

The Moel Bronymiod/Bwlch Mawr Upland Survey was carried out as two separate projects, examining an upland area on the north coast of the Llŷn Peninsula. The first survey, carried out over the autumn and winter of 1994-5 (Jones 1994), covered the southern part of the area, and the survey was completed in the autumn of 1997 (Geary 1998). The total survey area spanned some fourteen square kilometres, which included the hills of Gyrn Goch, Gyrn Ddu, Moel Bronymiod, Bwlch Mawr and Pen-y-gaer, all rising to between 400 metres and 500 metres above sea-level.

The principal reason for choosing this area for survey was that it represented a discrete block of upland landscape separate from the main mountainous ranges of Snowdonia and

Gyrn Ddu viewed from the south, showing the abandoned farm of Fron Heulog. G1488/06/24

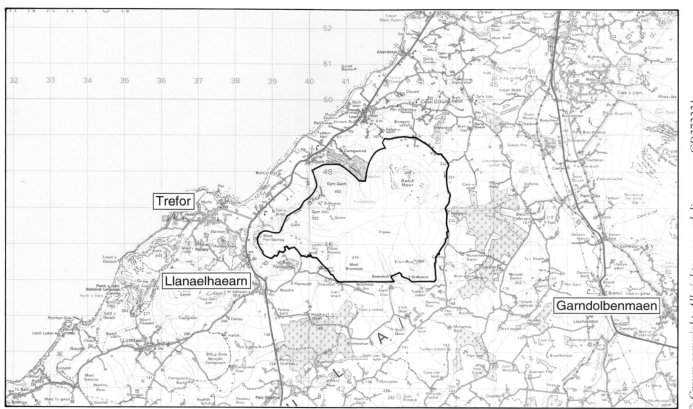

The Moel Bronymiod and Bwlch Mawr upland survey area in the Llŷn peninsula.

very different in character as a result. The survey zone also lay within the Llŷn Environmentally Sensitive Area, so the results of the survey could potentially be used to inform management regimes within the scheme.

At the outset of the survey the regional Sites and Monuments Record contained information on fifty-one archaeological sites, of which eight were scheduled as monuments of national importance. Reports from Cadw's field monument wardens, who visit scheduled sites, as well as from two of the local landowners suggested that the potential for adding to that number was high.

The landscape

The peaks which dominate the survey area form part of a series of igneous intrusions running the length of the Llŷn Peninsula, standing proud of the less resistant, sedimentary rock which surrounds them. The soils are generally poor and the vegetation consists mostly of moorland and rough pasture forming extensive upland sheepwalks. There is some encroachment of small improved fields, particularly on the north-eastern extent of the area, as well as complex, multi-period field systems along the eastern boundary and to the

Terraced fields to the south-west of Cae-hir Uchaf are surviving fragments of the medieval landscape. G1488/06/09 PRN 14503

south-west. Poor drainage has led to some particularly wet conditions over parts of the survey area, notably on either side of the Clipiau ridge, which runs across the middle of the survey area from west to east. The main areas of peat growth are found around Cors y Ddalfa and the eastern side of Gyrn Goch, but evidence for small-scale peat-cutting was widespread across the locality. Extensive areas of scree cover the slopes of all five hills, and the survey area as a whole is naturally very stony.

Results

As with all the Upland Survey projects the study of Moel Bronymiod/Bwlch Mawr dramatically increased the number of archaeological sites recorded within the area, in this case from fifty-one to eight hundred and thirty-two. Although this figure is primarily a result of the methodology of such an extensive field search, where all indications of past human activity are recorded, it provides the landscape context for a significant number of important new discoveries. The surveys looked at four main themes: settlement, agriculture, religious and funerary sites and industry.

Settlement

The survey area is now sparsely populated with just a few occupied farms scattered around the southern base of the hills, and a few small cottages on its northern edge. Evidently this was not always the case. Late-prehistoric settlement consisting of the remains of circular huts, either singly or in groups, seemed to occur most frequently in the south, although a poorer survival rate as a result of the encroachment of improved fields on the northern and coastal slopes may partially account for this distribution. In the south-west of the area in particular the settlements seemed to be associated with field systems, although the use, re-use and modification of the field boundaries in this area over at least two millennia have created a palimpsest that, in places, could not be unravelled by the eye alone. Somewhat surprisingly, the remains of settlements of prehistoric or Romano-British date were also found on the seemingly inhospitable western and north-western slopes of Gyrn Goch and Gyrn Ddu, in some particularly exposed locations on or above the 400 metres contour.

The small hillfort at Pen-y-gaer, on the south-eastern edge of the study area, occupies the top of an isolated hill. Its steeply sloping sides are defended by drystone walls, within which the remains of around a dozen terraced platforms are the only evidence of former houses.

Medieval settlement was particularly well represented within the locality, part of which is known to have lain within the medieval township of Cwm, in the commote of Uwch Gwyrfai. The township was granted to the Cistercian Order in the thirteenth century by Llywelyn ap Iorwerth, and farmed as a grange of the abbey of Aberconwy until the Dissolution of the Monasteries in the 1530s. Clawdd Seri, an earthen bank and ditch running across the Clipiau ridge, is thought to form part of the boundary of the grange.

The settlements of this period, characterised by the foundations of rectangular houses or long-huts, seem to occur in two main areas, although, again, we must consider the effects of later land improvement on the distribution of surviving remains. The first area seems to coincide broadly with the township of Cwm along the eastern edge of the survey zone. Here, a number of settlements survive between the 200-metre and the 280-metre contour. They may be the upper extents of a more widespread but fairly dispersed settlement, the remains lower down the slopes having been removed by later agriculture. A more complete fragment of the medieval landscape survives to the south-west of Cae-hir Uchaf, where a series of small fields, terraced into the slope and revetted by massive orthostatic walls, surrounds the remains of a substantial long-hut and a corn-drying kiln. However, without excavation it is impossible to date the settlements precisely or, indeed, to be even sure that they were all occupied at the same time.

The second area where medieval settlement remains survive is in the south-west, between Moel Penllechog and Moel Bronymiod. Above a complex multi-period field pattern the remains of what may have been medieval strip fields are still marked on the modern Ordnance Survey maps, just to the east of Fron Heulog. Earlier maps show these narrow fields extending to the east, below the trackway which runs roughly east-west across the middle of the survey area. Prehistoric, medieval and post-medieval settlements are fairly evenly distributed across this area, indicating a continuity of settlement and agriculture in this region unparalleled elsewhere in the neighbourhood.

Although a small number of the farms of the post-medieval centuries are still occupied the majority are abandoned. The settlement pattern changed again in recent centuries as the population shifted to the towns. The later farms range in date from about the seventeenth century to the nineteenth and early twentieth centuries and vary in form from roofless ruins to recently abandoned properties. As mixed farming has given way to a wholly pastoral economy, based largely on sheep farming, so the numbers of individual holdings have declined,

and this less intensive system has, in some measure, removed some of the threat to the settlement remains of the past.

Agriculture

Vestiges of settlement and agriculture are very closely associated in rural areas such as this where the former depended on the latter for its survival. Mention has already been made of the field systems associated with prehistoric and medieval settlements within the study area. Later agricultural features, including walls, sheepfolds and stock enclosures, formed the majority of the sites recorded during both surveys, and the current landscape strongly reflects the sheep-based agricultural system which has dominated the area since the eighteenth century. The enclosure of common land in the nineteenth century formed the large upland sheepwalks which characterise the area today, but the clearance and continued improvement of the small fields around its margins indicate the continuation of arable cultivation into recent centuries.

Distinctive features of the nineteenth-century enclosures are the mountain walls which march across the landscape, seemingly heedless of contour, altitude or topography. A number of small circular hollows discovered in the scree on the south- western slopes of Gyrn Ddu were interpreted as bivouacs, or shelters, associated with the construction of the mountain walls. During the worst weather of the survey it was easy to sympathise with the wall-builders for whom these shelters would have provided the only protection from the elements.

Religious and Funerary

The earliest evidence for human activity of any kind locally is in the form of ceremonial and burial monuments of the Bronze Age. Three standing stones were discovered in the south, and a number of burial cairns, also of presumed Bronze Age date, were recorded across the survey area. These latter included a group on the northern side of Cors y Ddalfa, which has been tentatively interpreted as a cemetery. Hilltop cairns were already recorded on Gyrn Ddu, with two groups located on plateaux to the south-west and to the east of the summit. A new discovery was the cairn just to the south-east of the summit of Bwlch Mawr. It appears similar in construction to the excavated cairn on the summit of nearby Tre'r Ceiri, better known for its hillfort. Unlike the Tre'r Ceiri cairn it has not suffered much disturbance, thanks to its remote location.

Industrial

Manganese mining to the south and east of the survey area and stone quarrying to the north-west form the basis of the industrial exploitation of the region during the nineteenth and early twentieth centuries. Manganese was mined on the Llŷn Peninsula from the late 1820s onwards (Griffith 1989), and the stone quarries of Gyrn Ddu were worked from 1864 until 1931, producing granite setts and macadam (Boyd 1981, 264-7).

Extensive evidence for peat-cutting was found across the area, but on a relatively small scale indicative of domestic exploitation. The valley to the north-east of Moel Bronymiod

On the eastern side of the survey area the contrast between the upland hill slopes and the valley bottom is particularly sharp. On the slopes traces of former field systems have survived obliteration by farming, forestry and land drainage. G1488/06/06 PRN 14503

was allotted to the poor of the parish of Llanaelhaearn when the area was enclosed (Bassett 1972, 146), and is recorded as 'Fuel Ground' on the 1839 tithe map.

Discussion

Changes in farming regimes from the eighteenth century onwards in the area have resulted in the survival of tantalising fragments of past landscapes from the late prehistoric period onwards, and two zones were identified as being ideal candidates for future study. The first of these, which follows the eastern boundary of the study area, is characterised by prehistoric settlement to the south merging with the medieval settlements which are a feature of the central part of the strip. Some of this area has subsequently been studied in more detail as part of a project to identify the medieval monastic landscape of the Cistercian grange of Cwm. Although the 'uplands' are identified as being above the 244-metre (800-foot) contour and, as a result, the surveys did not extend below that level, the 'cut-off' point has no relevance to the past landscapes being surveyed, and this area of medieval settlement was observed to extend to the east of the road which runs exactly north-south at this point. The date of the road and its relationship to the settlement remains might also make an interesting future study.

The second locality which might benefit from further study lies between Moel Penllechog and Moel Bronymiod. Medieval and later adaptation of prehistoric field systems has created a landscape of particular complexity here. The area occupies predominantly southerly- and south-westerly-facing slopes and is sheltered from almost all directions by the surrounding hills. It is no surprise, then, that this ground should have seen the greatest continuity of land-use of the entire study area, and there is great potential for future work here combining documentary research and environmental sampling with targeted excavation.

Y BERWYN

Robert Silvester (Clwyd-Powys Archaeological Trust)

Trekking along the summits that mould the central spine of Y Berwyn – Moel Sych, Cadair Berwyn, Cadair Fronwen, Cerrig Coediog and Moel Fferna – the walker can look out across two upland landscapes, at once both similar and different. To the west the moorlands, laced with small yet deeply cut valleys, fall away gently before tipping sharply to the plain occupied by the River Dee (Afon Dyfrdwy) and the valley of its tributary, Cwm Pennant; beyond are the northern reaches of the Cambrian Mountains, and behind those, Snowdonia. Eastwards the ridges and the valleys that separate them are more drawn out, running right up to the edge of the escarpment, but also offering a softer landscape that changes gradually from moorland to farmland, before descending to the levels of the Cheshire Plain.

On that central spine large summit cairns of Bronze Age date reveal human endeavours to memorialise the dead, but

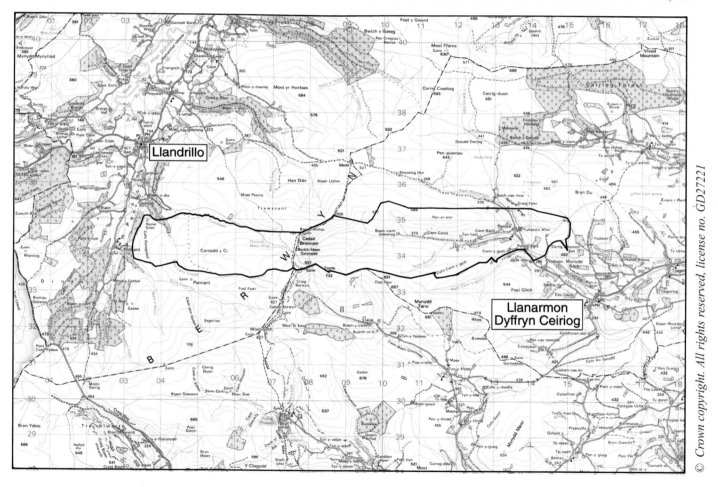

(above) Map of Y Berwyn project area, defining the area of survey in 1992 onwards.

(opposite) The different landscapes to either side of the central ridge are clearly visible in this aerial view of Y Berwyn, with the scarp slope and deeply incised valleys to the east and the more gentle dip slope to the west. Cadair Berwyn with its large cairn lying back a little from the lip of the escarpment is visible in the middle distance, while in the foreground a natural lake, Llŷn Lluncaws, fills the head of a valley below Moel Sych. 93-cs-0866

these are exceptional: Cadair Berwyn at 827 metres (2713 feet) above sea level is one of the highest peaks in Wales, and even Cerrig Coediog at 592 metres is well above the level where human activity on any scale might be anticipated. Rather it is at lower altitudes, on the periphery of the Berwyn and particularly in the valleys, where we might expect to identify the physical remains left by the communities who lived in sight of the mountainous ridge that dominates everything around it.

The field survey in 1992 examined an east-to-west transect, 1.5 kilometres wide, across the Berwyn from Pentre, north-west of the village of Llanarmon Dyffryn Ceiriog, to the higher reaches of Cwm Pennant in the west. The archaeological remains of the uplands on either side of the great ridge proved to be very different, and in more recent years several other smaller projects, some under the auspices of the Uplands Initiative, have examined more of the western edge of the Berwyns, revealing the richness and variety of its archaeology to such an extent that in 2001 the area was designated in the *Register of Landscapes of Special Historic Interest in Wales* (Cadw 2001, 2).

East of the mountain ridge

There can be little doubt that the ridges and valleys to the east of the main ridge were frequented in prehistoric times, even if traces are sparse. Cairns on some of the hills and ridges and the defended hilltop settlement at Cerrig Gwynion, just to the north of Llanarmon Dyffryn Ceiriog, signal extensive prehistoric activity, although in the transect survey little of that period could be identified. A possible prehistoric hut circle, revealed as a ring-bank of stone, represents the total of the discoveries, for much of the transect area has been enclosed and pasture improvement is likely to have erased many earlier traces. Indeed, what appears to have been a sub-circular enclosure of likely late prehistoric date, on a south-facing slope above Nant Cwm-llawenog, appears on an aerial photograph of 1946, but more recent agricultural activity has left only an amorphous platform which tells us little about its origins.

Along the valley of Nant Cwm-llawenog the survey recorded earthworks relating to settlement and agriculture, ostensibly of post-medieval origin, although some might go back into the medieval centuries. One or two of the still-occupied farms could, for instance, have been established in the late Middle Ages, even though the buildings now visible are clearly more recent. However, the platforms and other earthworks, and the stone-built sheepfolds, are much more

likely to date from a time when seasonal use of the hills was commonplace, perhaps from the end of the medieval period through to the seventeenth century or even later. These are also hills that were shared out between the great Denbighshire landowners, and the incised boundary stones on the tops of the ridges are marked with WWW and M or CC on opposing faces, indicating where the lands of Watkin Williams-Wynn of Wynnstay gave way to those of the Myddleton family of Chirk Castle (Castell Y Waun).

West of the mountain ridge

The upper Dee (Afon Dyfrdwy) valley where it edges the western and northern sides of the Berwyn massif displays some spectacular prehistoric funerary and ritual monuments, particularly in the vicinity of the village of Llandrillo-yn-Rhos, where the Ceidiog stream running down Cwm Pennant enters the main river. While several of these monuments lie close to the Dee itself, the kerb circle on Moel Ty Uchaf (Bowen and Gresham 1967) occupies one of the more westerly of the Berwyn summits and, with a number of other cairns on the east side of Cwm Pennant, including an exceptionally fine cairn composed of three circular bands of small stones, reflects the importance of this area to local Bronze Age communities. This is emphasised by some of the new discoveries, for within a one-kilometre radius of that triple ring cairn are at least ten other burial cairns, all showing some evidence of structural complexity, whether it be a surrounding kerb of large blocks or an internal cist, and yet other, totally formless, cairns which may have been funerary in origin, but cannot now be distinguished from clearance cairns indicative of agriculture.

It is not only the dead that are represented above Cwm Pennant. Surviving on a natural terrace and not far from the lip of the valley is a small and rather denuded sub-circular hut set within a D-shaped configuration of scarp banks and fringed by the lynchets of a later age (see below), the visible remains suggesting a small, prehistoric house-site within its own enclosure or pound. Later activity has inflicted less damage on the prehistoric remains on the open moorland, for the spur referred to above has not only the burial cairns, but also a settlement area. The focus of this is the grass-covered, rubble foundations of a large circular house, some 10 metres in diameter, with its entrance on the east side. Surrounding it on all sides is a fragmented network of 'wandering walls', low banks of tumbled stone meandering across the spur and thought to define 'fields', relatively level areas which have

Possibly dating from the third millennium BC, the kerb circle on Moel Ty Uchaf survives in heavily improved pasture on a gentle summit of the western Berwyns above the village of Llandrillo. Large stones sharply define the circle, but unrecorded excavations, probably in the nineteenth century, have removed most of what may have been a central burial. Several other small cists and stones are set a few metres away from the circle, but cannot be satisfactorily distinguished from the air. 95-cs-0217

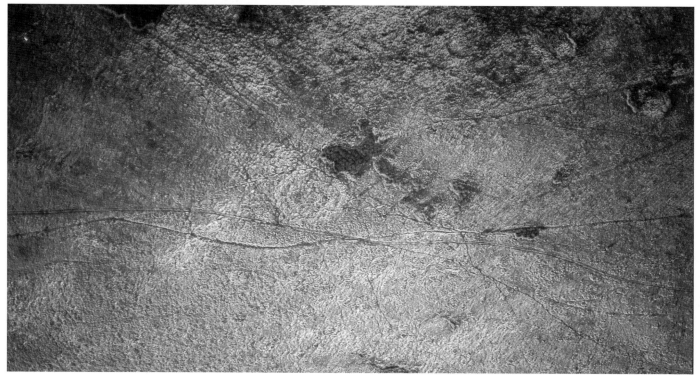

Highlighted by a light covering of snow are the concentric rings of a fine structured cairn, some 20 metres in diameter. The two outermost rings are the most obvious, while the innermost, hardly visible in the photo, may actually be the remains of a denuded central cairn. This is perhaps the most impressive of a significant group of cairns dispersed above the eastern slopes of Cwm Pennant in Llandrillo. A second, smaller, cairn can be seen above and to the left of the main one. 2001-cs-1603

Medieval strip fields below Cefn Penagored show as linear banks of grass-covered rubble, some of them later re-used as bases for more modern field boundaries. In the bottom left of the photograph the banks are much less obvious, a result of agricultural clearance associated with a post-medieval farm just out of picture. Just above the centre point of the photo are the traces of a rectangular enclosure which contains a hafod superimposed on the earlier fields. 95-cs-0055

been cleared of surface stone. The most prominent wall, incorporating slabs deliberately set on edge, divides the 'fields' from the slopes which are littered with small dumps of stone. More than forty of these clearance cairns have been recorded, and others may have escaped attention because of the difficulty of distinguishing less prominent scatters from naturally occurring spreads of surface debris. A second hut circle, a much smaller structure, is set against the south face of one of the walls, and a third feature, either a hut or perhaps another ring cairn, is largely overlain by a circular sheepfold (see below). Quite possibly, although this has not been proved by excavation, the agricultural settlement was contemporary with at least some of the nearby cairns.

When extensive remains of long strip fields were first recognised on the edge of Y Berwyn above Llandrillo on aerial photographs taken in 1982 they too were thought to be of prehistoric date, a view which has not been entirely eradicated even today (Cadw 2001, 2). Fieldwork, however, has clearly demonstrated that these field systems, possibly the most extensive upland agricultural systems of their kind in Wales, are of medieval origin (Silvester 2000). Those below Cefn Penagored are the most extensive, formerly spreading over at

least sixty-five hectares, those on neighbouring Ffridd Camen the best preserved, and it is evident from aerial photography that field systems of the same general form once extended for nearly seven kilometres along the eastern edge of the Ceidiog and Dee (Dyfrdwy) valleys.

Some of the fields are more than 400 metres long, running down the slopes and perpendicular to the grain of the land before swinging through a right-angle to follow the contours as the ground steepens into the Ceidiog valley, creating a classic pattern of lynchets and terraces. Cultivation ridges are also present, though only sporadically. However, the most important association is with the earthworks of the house sites that accompany the fields, confirming unequivocally their medieval origin. Most of these earthworks show as long platforms cut back into the slope, and some of them display the foundations of rectangular buildings. The relationship between houses and fields is most marked on Rhyd Gethin hill, where two pairs of platforms lie at the end of field boundary banks. Rarer, on level ground, are the remains of buildings without any accompanying earthworks. The foundations of what was perhaps a true long-house, where human and animals were accommodated at opposite ends of the same building, lie beneath a rock outcrop on Ffridd Camen, and it is set centrally to a block of strip fields which is laid out below it.

In later centuries this western face of the Berwyns was occupied on both a seasonal and a permanent basis. Scattered on the slopes and along the valleys is a number of small rectangular structures which undoubtedly functioned as *hafodydd*. From Trum y Wern southwards to Crechwyl, a distance of five kilometres, fifteen such sites have been identified. One, on the western slopes below Cefn Penagored, is exceptional in that it is set in improved pasture, its survival almost certainly due to its containment within a stone-walled pound which acted as a deterrent to later agricultural clearance and instead became a repository for clearance stone; we can only suspect that others in comparable positions have almost certainly been less leniently treated. Two types of site are apparent. Those on valley floors are normally found in isolated locations without any associated features; they are sheltered and have a nearby water supply that could be utilised, but the valley sides frequently restrict wide views of the grazing grounds. In contrast, there are a number of similar buildings in more open spots – on spurs or close to the upper edges of valleys – with wider aspects. Some, though not all of these, have surrounding or appended enclosures, mostly small, except for one above Nant Esgeiriau which extends over an area of nearly 0.35 of a hectare. The distribution of these seasonal settlements is geographically limited: with the exception of one high up the valley of Clochnant, nearly three kilometres from the Cwm Pennant, but even then set at no more than 450 metres above sea-level, most are less than two kilometres from the valley and at heights rarely of much more than 400 metres above sea-level. Thus it appears that from the point of view of summer pasturage the gentler lower slopes of the Berwyns provided sufficient grazing for the local communities that exploited the hills. At 500 metres high, and in places at even lower altitudes, blanket peat with heather and bilberry replaces the grass; stock may have grazed on this vegetation, but the *hafod* sites avoided it. What is clear is that after the demise of the permanent medieval settlements and their fields, perhaps as a result of climatic change and plague in the fourteenth century, and perhaps too because of changing social conditions, the western flanks of the Berwyns witnessed a reversion to summer activity only, possibly for two or three hundred years (Silvester 2000, 55).

The stone foundations of a rectangular building, perhaps a hafod, are set down the slope adjacent to Nant Esgeiriau, one of the tributary streams that feed into Cwm Pennant, and are provided with some shelter by the rising valley sides to south (to the left) and north. This building, however, is more sophisticated than many of its kind, for a cross-passage at the near end creates two compartments, while a porch projects near the far corner, just right of centre on the photograph. The building is situated within its own enclosure (not visible), which would have facilitated the control of stock. 2002-0053-4

Amongst the most common features of the uplands from the last two to three centuries are those linked to the pasturing of sheep. Sheepfolds can take many forms, but circular examples such as this one, lying well to the east of Cwm Pennant, are unusual. Furthermore, the occasional stones that project through the turf beyond the fold wall suggest that its builders may have utilised rubble from an already existing structure, perhaps a prehistoric ring cairn. In the foreground just to the left of centre is the base of a small rectangular shelter that may have been used by a shepherd. 2002-0052-12

It thus took some considerable time for the permanent recolonisation of the Berwyns' edge, and there is in fact only a solitary example of a post-medieval farm on the western edge. This had ceased to function by the mid-nineteenth century. It consists of the ruins of two buildings, one the farmhouse itself, the other which is adjacent, presumably an ancillary structure such as a barn. The entire holding is surrounded by a dry-stone wall and sub-divided into about nine smaller enclosures by low earthwork banks, sometimes accompanied by shallow ditches; two or three of these enclosures can probably be classed as garden plots or paddocks. Scattered throughout the fields are cairns of cleared stone, almost certainly contemporary with the farmstead. As the only landholding on this upland edge its utilisation of the spur slopes between the Ceidiog and its tributary and its position on a north-facing break of slope overlooking the valley and within sight of the village of Llandrillo point to a cautious development, but one that ultimately failed.

Surviving evidence of other forms of exploitation of the moorland edge over the last couple of hundred years is rather more widespread. Stock-grazing manifests itself in the sheepfolds and shelters, and each valley has a fold complex, in use until recently. The circular fold on the spur mentioned above, with an internal diameter of nearly 6 metres and two

antenna walls running off from the entrance to funnel stock into it, is unusual and reminiscent of the similarly shaped and relatively modern sheep stells of the Scottish borders. While it is legitimate to wonder whether it betrays the Scottish links of its builder, its appearance on an Ordnance Survey surveyor's drawing of 1831/2 precludes any association with Henry Robertson, a man of Scottish origin, who purchased this estate on the western edge of the Berwyns in 1869.

The rectilinear depressions left by peat-cutting on the high ridges of Carnedd y Ci and above Pennant and Yr Aran confirm Samuel Lewis's statement in 1833 that in Llandrillo 'peat is procured in great quantities for fuel'. Several quarries were also opened up on the Berwyns' slopes. One above Ffridd Camen was certainly the source of the slate slabs used for the wall surrounding the *ffridd* (an upland intake), but, more significantly, a feeder track from the quarry continued through the *ffridd*, forded the Clochnant stream, and continued down to the farms in the valley of the Ceidiog, for which it is known to have produced stone in 1834. A larger quarry with extensive waste tips on the north bank of Nant Cwm Tywyll may have originated in the early eighteenth century; it, too, has tracks for both carts and pack-horses leading from it towards the gentler exit provided by the Nant Esgeiriau valley. The latter site is probably 'the quarry of excellent slate' on the Berwyn mountain referred to by Lewis (1833). Grouse shooting has been an attraction here for nearly two centuries, sale particulars for the Hendwr Estate, whose centre lay on the Dee plain, claiming it to be 'the equal at least to any in Wales..'. At least two lines of shooting butts, probably of later nineteenth-century or even more recent date, have been identified. Finally, the estate was almost certainly responsible for the establishment of the pine plantation set within a ring bank on top of Nurse Gron. Traditionally it commemorated the victory at Waterloo, and it remains an exceptional landmark when viewed from the valley below.

There are marked differences in both the nature and the density of archaeological and historic landscape remains on either side of the central Berwyn ridge. On the west prehistoric, medieval and even post-medieval activity is concentrated quite tightly on the uplands immediately above the valleys of the Dee and its tributary. Not that this is a surprise, but it does signal the considerable potential for the rest of this western edge of the Berwyns, which has yet to be examined. East of the ridge the archaeology is more diffuse, and arguably the discoveries more predictable, a result of the fact that the agricultural zones that have been exploited in the past stretch along the ridges and the valleys between.

MYNYDD EPYNT:
REDISCOVERING AN ABANDONED FARMING LANDSCAPE

Toby Driver (Royal Commission on the Ancient and Historical Monuments of Wales) and Robert Silvester (Clwyd-Powys Archaeological Trust)

Introduction

Mynydd Epynt is a desolate tract of upland plateau in central southern Wales, one of a number of extremely high and remote moorlands towards the southern edge of the Cambrian Mountains that stretch between the Brecon Beacons in the south and the grey peaks of Snowdonia in the north. This bare plateau is dotted with small ponds and peat bogs and is deeply dissected along its southern fringes by numerous river valleys, among them those of the Honddu, Brân and Cilieni. A great

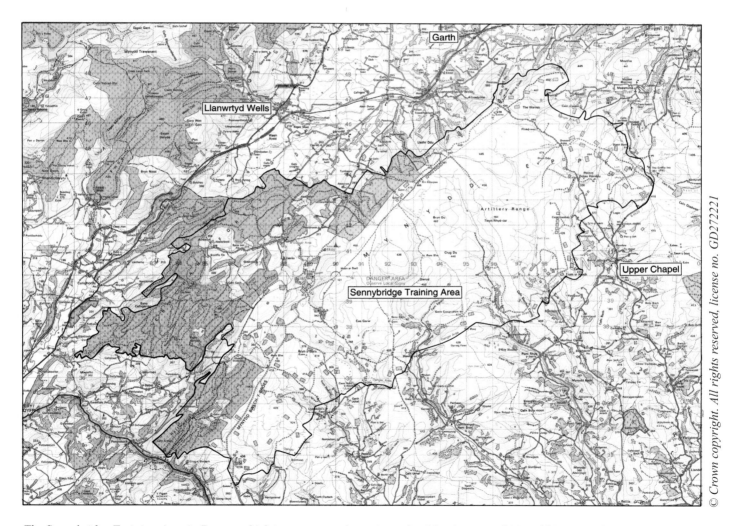

The Sennybridge Training Area in Powys, which incorporates the major upland landmasses of Mynydd Epynt in the central and north-east part and Mynydd Bwlch-y-Groes in the south-west part, with the Crychan Forest in the west. The upland plateau is bordered along the north side by a steep escarpment and is fringed along its southern edges by a series of minor river valleys draining to the south and south-west. RCAHMW

escarpment falls away along the north edge to the valley of the Irfon, and north-east to the route of the Wye.

Epynt was requisitioned in 1939 by the Ministry of Defence (MoD) for military training, and remains in use today as the Sennybridge Training Area – for a history of the range see Church 1990. The greater proportion of Mynydd Epynt, some 196 square kilometres in extent, forms a restricted military 'Impact Area' used for live firing and training. To the south-west Mynydd Bwlch y Groes is a continuing ridge of high ground also used for training, eventually broken by the deep valley of the Afon Gwydderig and the main Brecon-Llandovery road. To the north-west is the dense post-war conifer plantation of Crychan Forest. Yet despite its comparative remoteness, Epynt is fringed by fertile lowlands and a number of important market towns, including Llandovery, Brecon, Builth Wells and Llanwrtyd Wells. Together these have helped contribute to rich droving and farming traditions on Epynt, and the enclosure of all but the most exposed upland moors with a network of historic farmsteads and field systems.

This paper describes two of the most recent surveys of the archaeology and history of Mynydd Epynt, each quite different to the other in its approach and yielding different results. The first took place in 1996-7, when the Royal Commission on the Ancient and Historical Monuments of Wales (RCAHMW) carried out air-photo mapping of the whole of the Sennybridge Training Area. Interpretation of hundreds of vertical aerial photographs yielded nearly seven hundred archaeological sites dating from prehistoric times to the end of the Second World War. Over four hundred of these had never before been recognised, including seventy-two farmsteads, forty-six pillow mounds (artificial warrens built for rabbit farming), and even seventeen systems of twentieth-century military practice trenches. The true value of the survey lay in the 're-population' of what had previously appeared to be a bleak and largely featureless landscape. It was now possible to see the homes and farms of the Epynt people, complete with field patterns, well-worn trackways and traces of rural industries, including peat-cutting and stone quarrying. The air-photo mapping provided a first glimpse at the complexity of this historic upland landscape and demonstrated the potential for more targeted ground investigation.

Following air-photo mapping a second study was carried out by the Clwyd-Powys Archaeological Trust (CPAT) as part of a wider assessment of deserted rural settlements in Brecknock, funded by Cadw: Welsh Historic Monuments. Several valleys on Epynt were visited by field archaeologists to assess the survival of medieval and later houses and farmsteads. Although some had already been recognised from aerial photographs, a significant number of new sites was discovered, shedding light on many centuries of settlement on Epynt. In places entirely new groups of medieval houses, farms and agricultural enclosures were recorded, hidden deep in sheltered valleys and on hill slopes. In combination these two surveys illustrate the wider benefits and drawbacks of both aerial and ground approaches in mapping and understanding human activity in the Welsh uplands.

Researching the history of Epynt

Many memories of life as it was on Epynt have been fondly collected over the years by local historians, among them the late Ronald Davies, author of *Epynt Without People*, and Herbert Hughes, author of *'Mae'n Ddiwedd Byd Yma…'* and *An Uprooted Community: A History of Epynt*. Prior to our recent work archaeological investigations on Epynt had been limited. Gerald C. Dunning excavated the stone circle and cairn at Ynyshir in 1940 (Dunning 1943; RCAHMW 1997, 101-2; 155-7), but it was not until the involvement of Dr Stephen Briggs of RCAHMW during the 1970s and 1980s, working with the MoD's Conservation Group, that a database of the old settlements and related features was first compiled in a systematic manner. Subsequent surveys of the prehistoric remains on Epynt were published in two parts as Volume 1 of the RCAHMW's Brecknock Inventory (RCAHMW 1986; 1997). The defunct military structures on the range are also of great interest and include shooting ranges, targets, trench systems and observation posts. Through the work of Stephen Briggs, the military historian Mark Khan (1995), and MoD staff including Jonathan Jackson, Assistant Range Officer until 2001, many remains have been documented for posterity.

Epynt – an historic landscape

The earliest traces of human habitation on Epynt are prehistoric burial and ritual monuments, most of which are presumed to date from the Early Bronze Age (c.2100 BC – 1500 BC). These include many fine round barrows like Tri Chrugiau (RCAHMW 1997, 104), and the Ynyshir stone circle. Both are protected as Scheduled Ancient Monuments. A defensive earthwork, Clawdd British, survives in the north-west of the area and has been variously ascribed an Iron Age or medieval origin (King 1961, 94; RCAHMW 1986, 22-3). The Romans left no discernible traces of roads or forts on Epynt, although the remains of marching camps, practice works, a road and a fortlet on Mynydd Bach Trecastell, nearby

A typical landscape in the heart of Epynt along the Cilieni valley, about three kilometres north of Llandeilo'r-Fan. This view shows a pattern of historic enclosure fields in the foreground giving way in the middle distance to unenclosed upland moor, actually the present-day boundary of the live-firing 'Impact Area' of the military range. A small prehistoric enclosure can be seen in the foreground to the right of the hedge. The most obvious and dramatic development in the landscape is the FIBUA Village ('Fighting in Built-Up Area'), a purpose-built training facility opened in 1990, based on a typical small West German village. It remains a striking and unexpected addition to the skyline of Mynydd Epynt. 98-cs-598

to the south-west, is a remarkable group (RCAHMW 1986, 150-3). The so-called Dark Ages and medieval periods are poorly understood, although recent fieldwork has shed some light on settlements dating to the latter period.

Mynydd Epynt is special in that it preserves a remarkably intact farming landscape broadly dating from the seventeenth to the early twentieth centuries, but with many more ancient elements. This preservation is in part due to the enforced evacuation of some fifty-four families from their homes and farms in 1939, with their re-location elsewhere in Brecknocks and beyond. While this event had a huge social impact, Briggs (1994, 14) has been keen to stress that it was in fact the culmination of an ongoing process of depopulation '…in which something probably approaching twice that number of properties had been deserted'. However, with the subsequent military stewardship the deserted landscape was unwittingly preserved through to the present day. The fragile traces of a lost way of life have been spared the advances of modern farming and upland 'improvement' which have eroded or erased comparable remains in many other Welsh uplands.

Military training on Epynt was the priority in the immediate post-war period, and historical buildings and archaeological earthworks were not always treated sympathetically. However, a far more enlightened approach to conservation matters since the 1980s has seen a number of initiatives designed actively to preserve and promote its history. Old farms are being sympathetically restored and hedgerows replanted, both having benefits for military training. This training remains the priority, but the new Integrated Land Management Plan for the Sennybridge Training Area recognises the value of the natural and historic built environment. In its words: 'It is the very scale of abandonment and survival of settlement, industrial and other features on the Epynt which make it such an interesting area for archaeology today' (Defence Estates 2001).

Mapping the landscape – the aerial photographic survey

Air-photo mapping was introduced as a method of landscape survey for the Royal Commission in Wales in 1995, following many successful years of national archaeological mapping in England (Bewley 1997). Stephen Briggs's work on Epynt had already demonstrated great potential for further archaeological survey, and the boundaries of the Sennybridge Training Area were chosen for the project. Vertical air photographs formed virtually the sole source for the mapping. These photographs

Waun-fawr farm in the Cilieni valley, with the FIBUA Village on the skyline beyond. This is typical of some conversions of historic farms to training facilities in the post-war years. More recent conversions have been far more sympathetic to the appearance of the original building and its setting in the landscape. 2002-cs-4000

are usually taken in long, continuous runs with a substantial overlap, allowing pairs of prints to be studied stereoscopically. This three-dimensional 'virtual' view showed the landscape as it was forty to sixty years ago, allowing a very high level of detail on the final mapping. The entire range area of 236 square kilometres was mapped and recorded by one person in eighty-four days, with every site given an accurate plan and written description. The results were compiled in an unpublished report lodged in the National Monuments Record of Wales (Driver 1997), and in a shorter, published paper (Driver 1998).

Building a picture of the landscape

A long-held view of Epynt has been that it is a remote and impoverished landscape, devoid of good farming land and poorly suited to settlement. A visit to the range on a windy and rain-lashed day can still confirm such impressions. Colyer (1984, 126-7) provides a dramatic and pessimistic view: 'Despite the panoramic views it offers, the Epynt is a dull, treeless and gloomy place brightened only by sinister red warning flags and enlivened by the occasional rattle of gunfire.'. King (1961, 94) described the enigmatic earthwork at Clawdd British as standing '…well away from cultivation, amid the howling desolation of Sennybridge artillery range.'. In fact the recent air- photo mapping clearly demonstrates that this site is not very far from traces of ridge and furrow cultivation, abandoned farms and fields, and areas of quarrying and peat cutting. Briggs describes the traditional way of life prior to the evacuation time as '…still based upon the small-scale mixed farming economy, mechanisation being generally limited to horse-drawn traction, with some dependence on water power' (Briggs 1994, 13). Few metalled roads existed on Epynt prior to military use, with many of the remote farms along the Ysgir Fechan and Ysgir Fawr valleys in the heart of Epynt connected by well-worn trackways over the hills. However, this did not prevent communications with the outside world; Epynt is famed in droving history, with Tafarn-y-Mynydd and the Drovers Arms being two famous stops on the high moors (Colyer 1984, 126-7; Davies 1984, 38-47).

One of the great strengths of the aerial perspective in the uplands is the ability to see very faint earthwork features such as old ploughed fields and trackways. Areas of relict ploughing in the heart of Epynt along the Ysgir Fawr valley were seen with striking clarity on winter photography from 1960. These confirmed that conditions were once favourable enough at the 400-metre contour for ploughing to advance high onto the hill slopes above the farms. To see such features

A low-level view of an un-named historic farmstead along the upper reaches of the Ysgir Fawr, with the remains of two stone long-houses among a group of small field enclosures. Traces of plough-cultivation can be seen within the larger fields on the hillside beyond. This and other aerial views were taken from a military Gazelle helicopter, loaned by the Ministry of Defence for a morning's archaeological reconnaissance in 1998 as part of survey work for the Integrated Land Management Plan. 98-cs-0629

Archaeology in the Welsh uplands takes all forms. Here a concrete drainage culvert built by Italian prisoners of war in 1945 survives on the Sennybridge Training Area and is a fascinating example of military history. The raised inscription '573 1945 PoW' shows the number of their original company. 2002-cs-4002

on the ground can be virtually impossible even on a good, clear winter's day with close-cropped grass and raking light. The hills bordering the Ysgir Fawr are largely covered by rough moorland grass and bracken, set aside for live-firing exercises, meaning that aerial photography is the only source which can show us the true extent of historic cultivation today.

Ysgir Fawr was one of the richest valleys for the air-photo mapping programme. Although the Ordnance Survey had, at the end of the nineteenth century, mapped the main field boundaries and houses of the larger farms like Byllfa-uchaf at the head of the valley and two substantial farms set off a tributary near Pwll Cam, much remained unrecorded. North of Pwll Ffrwd a finely preserved farmstead was found on the valley floor, its boundary fence enclosing both the more fertile soils alongside the river and a tract of moorland above for grazing livestock. A single long-house represented the dwelling, while a series of well-marked ridges on the valley floor was probably a rudimentary set of water meadows, where winter floodwater would be encouraged over the plots to deposit fertile river silts. Unexpected sites were also mapped: two simple 'D'-shaped enclosures, some 40 metres across,

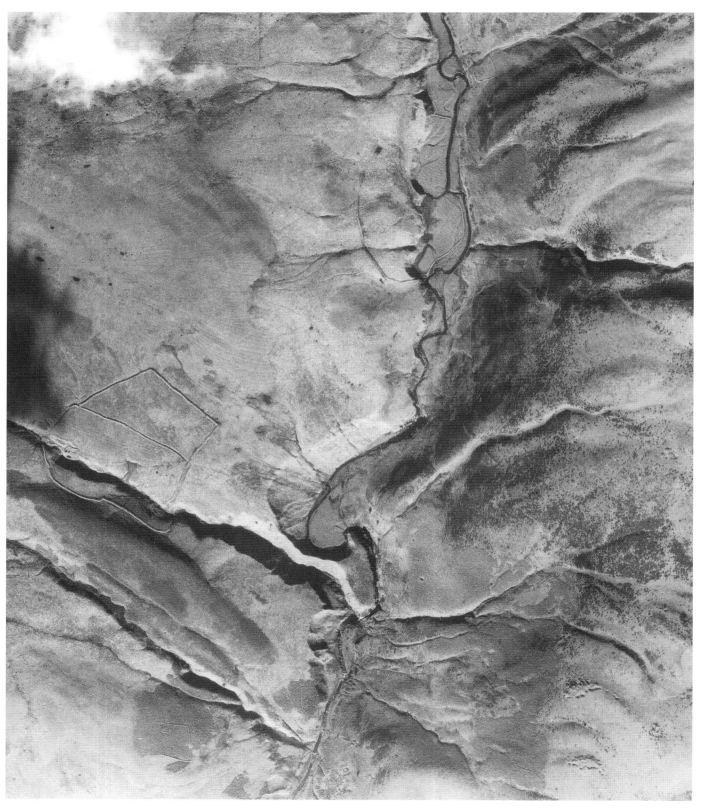

were noticed in promontory positions overlooking the steep valley sides of the Ysgir Fawr, south of Pwll Frwd. Although these may be historic farmsteads or sheepfolds, their defensive position suggests an origin in the prehistoric Iron Age.

Understanding house and farm – the ground survey of Epynt

The assessment of the evidence seen on aerial photography offers a starting point for the analysis of any landscape, and in the case of the vast upland tracts of Epynt the remains of past farming activity become very clear. The patterns of cultivation and enclosure, the trackways, the leats and other watercourses all become more intelligible when seen from an aerial perspective, and from the photographs a map can be produced depicting the relationships. This, though, is only a first step in reading the landscapes of the past. Much more can be seen on the ground: features too small or too indistinct to register clearly on high-level photographs, and details and subtleties which simply cannot be picked up from standard aerial photographs.

In the upper reaches of the Ysgir Fechan valley the post-medieval farmsteads of Beili-Richard, Rhyd-y-maen and Car create a continuous zone of enclosures and fields along the floor and sides of the valley, and even higher up are the isolated farms of Cwm-car and Cwm-tylciau, the latter so remote that it reflects an optimistic yet futile attempt to establish a farm at the head of the valley in the second half of the nineteenth century. All these are shown on modern maps, but the aerial photograph analysis has added details of associated cultivation, enclosure and quarrying. However, not everything shows. In a little

Vertical aerial photograph of the Ysgir Fawr valley in the heart of Mynydd Epynt. Taken in 1960, this view shows the very core of the military Impact Area to which aerial and ground access is restricted for most of the year. The low November light picks out the earthworks of old farms and ploughed fields to perfection. When a pair of adjacent vertical images are viewed together in stereo the archaeologist can study a 'virtual' landscape, seeing valleys, hills and archaeological features in three dimensions. Crown Copyright 1960/MoD ref. F43 58/RAF/3916, 0201

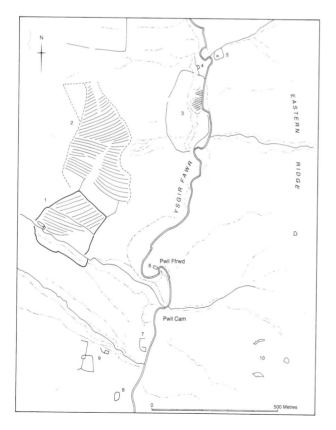

Interpretation of the Ysgir Fawr vertical photograph.

1. Large farmstead of post-medieval date, which spans a tributary of the Ysgir Fawr.

2. Area of cultivation: the intact ridges and furrows of old ploughed fields are still visible in this remarkable view, yet would be extremely difficult to identify at ground level in tussocky grass or bracken.

3. Farmstead on the floor of the Ysgir Fawr, with a large boundary bank enclosing part of the valley, which then runs up onto the moorland. A rectangular long-house (4) can also be seen. Lines of plough cultivation can be seen on the valley floor.

5. Agricultural enclosure with a small structure within, perhaps a long-house.

6. Rectangular long-house on the floor of the valley above the waterfall at Pwll Ffrwd.

7. and 8. Two promontory enclosures. Settlements are usually placed on the edges of promontories for the purposes of defence, and we might expect these sites to be prehistoric forts. However, their size and form make it more likely they date from recent centuries and were associated with farming settlement or stock management. The reason for their precarious positioning remains a mystery.

9. Farmstead with a paddock alongside, and another long-house to the north-east.

10. Disused tilestone quarries on Eastern Ridge, perhaps periodically worked by the farmers living in the valley below.

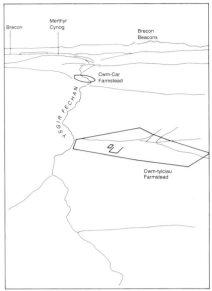

The desolate landscape in the uppermost reaches of the Ysgir Fechan, looking south to the peaks of the Brecon Beacons in the far distance. The remains of the remote Cwm-tylciau farm can be seen in the right middle-distance. 98-cs-0703

valley where a tributary of the Ysgir Fechan runs in from the west, just above the enclosed land of Car farm, are several small long-huts, identified first by the assistant range warden but not apparent on aerial photographs. Spaced out almost regularly on the valley floor these simple 8- to 9-metres-long huts probably represent *hafodydd* or *lluestai*, the summer houses of upland graziers from a time before permanent farming spread up the main valley.

The valley of Blaen Duhonw lies close to the northern fringe of Epynt, but the course of this stream northwards to the

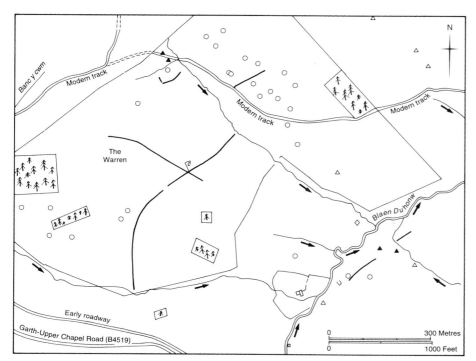

Key
▲ Long-huts (Aerial Discovery)
△ Long-huts (Ground Discovery)
◇ Platforms (Ground Discovery)
○ Pillow Mounds (Aerial Discovery)
╲ Boundary Banks (Aerial Discovery)

The Warren, Epynt: this comparative plan shows the pillow mounds, longhouses and other features discovered and mapped from aerial photography, together with the additional house platforms and long-houses missed in the original work but subsequently identified on the ground. RCAHMW drawing

River Irfon is interrupted by a high ridge known variously as Banc y Cwm and The Warren, and instead it is deflected eastwards to join the Wye. Towards the head of this stream early maps mark the now abandoned farmstead of Dolaugwynion and several sheepfolds, while the warren name, clearly pointing to rabbit farming in the locality, was confirmed by the aerial photograph analysis which picked up thirty-four pillow mounds. The aerial photographs also displayed, in addition to Dolau-gwynion, two long-huts on a flat spur between converging streams.

Fieldwork fleshes out this farming picture. On the opposite side of the stream to the abandoned farm is a large platform on which once a dwelling probably stood. Little is left of the building – only a few upright slabs – but it is tempting to view this as a predecessor of Dolau-gwynion, its building material robbed to construct the later farm or its outbuildings. To the two long-huts downstream two further examples can be added, but it is on the slopes below the warren that major discoveries have been made. Four large platforms, one of them more than 30 metres long with the remnants of a rectangular building on it, nearly 20 metres long, lie on the south- and east-facing slopes. One of these might perhaps be the site of the eighteenth- or nineteenth-century house of the warren keeper, but the others could represent earlier dwellings, perhaps of the medieval era.

Finally we can turn to Pant-y-blodau, an enclosure and platform tentatively identified as the site of a building from the aerial photography, but difficult to see amongst the surface stone strewn across the slope. This shows on the ground as a small rectangular house-site about 8.5 metres long, it walls comprising upright slabs retaining rubble fill. Around this was a stone-banked enclosure, and also within its perimeter was a sunken, stone-lined store for keeping dairy products cool. Two earthen clamps which may have served a similar purpose for other agricultural products lie just outside the enclosure.

Tir-cyd – a surprise of national importance

During 1999 the local historian Glyn Evans contacted Toby Driver regarding some 'stone circles' found on the southern fringe of Epynt. A farmer friend, Mr Prosser, from Llanfihangel Nant Brân had noted several settings of upright stones on a hillside near Tir-cyd just to the north. During a site visit it became clear that, unlike what might be expected of a prehistoric ritual site, the upright stones were arranged in two rectangles and were actually the footing walls of two houses. Upright slabs formed the inner and outer wall faces, with larger stones used at the corners and as door jambs. Some metres away was a substantial house platform shelved into the hillslope, the remains of a very well preserved farmstead similar to the best examples recorded elsewhere on the range, while the stone-built huts appear to be from a different phase

95

of occupation. The site had been mapped from aerial photographs in 1997, but thick vegetation and hill shadow had obscured many of the features. Tir-cyd was fully surveyed by the Clwyd-Powys Archaeological Trust and was subsequently designated as a Scheduled Ancient Monument by Cadw, in recognition of its exceptional preservation. Given the history of fieldwork and survey on Epynt by professional archaeologists it was good to know that the keen eyes of a local farmer still had much to offer. Unlike many of the other surveys recorded in this volume, the fieldwork that has so far been completed on Mynydd Epynt cannot be classed as systematic, but on the basis of what has been done we can assume many more sites remain to be found and recorded.

Conclusions

In management terms the timing of the air-photo mapping and ground surveys on Mynydd Epynt has been fortuitous. In 2001 the MoD completed a four-year Integrated Land Management Plan for the Sennybridge Range, a programme of data-

Pant-y-blodau deserted rural settlement, above the Cilieni valley. The remains of a long-house with stone foundations (seen in this view) survive within a rectangular enclosure and may date from the medieval period. The complex is now a Scheduled Ancient Monument. 2002-cs-4001

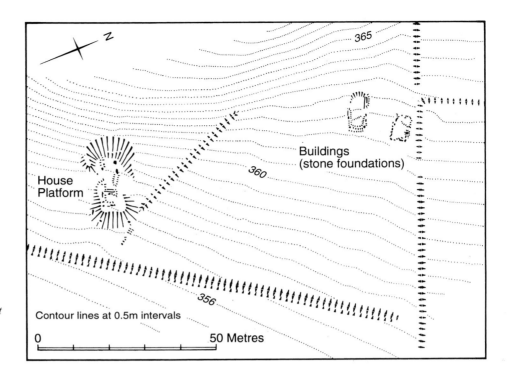

Plan of the deserted rural settlement at Tir Cyd, now a Scheduled Ancient Monument. After Clwyd-Powys Archaeological Trust/Cadw drawing

gathering and survey to assess all resources which require management or protection. The archaeological report published from the mapping provided the MoD with a first-level index for their archaeological resource, building on the existing sites and monuments record. The subsequent fieldwork considerably enhanced the understanding of Epynt historically. With the statutory protection of three deserted rural settlements (among them Pant-y-blodau and Tir-cyd) as Scheduled Ancient Monuments of national importance, together with the opening of the Disgwylfa visitor centre in a restored historic farmhouse, enormous progress has been made in recording, understanding and conserving the traces of Epynt's farming history.

The analysis of aerial photography represented a first stage in mapping the historic landscape of Epynt, and is now a routine preliminary to any field survey funded through the Uplands Initiative. The overall picture, and indeed its elucidation, then required elaboration through detailed fieldwork and interpretation of the remains. We should realise that Epynt is not one but several landscapes, the most recent of which, the military one, is not only very different from those of the past but is still in the process of being created. Much work remains to be done, but it is only with a combined approach that a better understanding can be achieved of how Epynt has been used by past generations of farming communities.

Further information

Aerial photography, plans and written records about the Mynydd Epynt surveys can be freely consulted at the National Monuments Record of Wales (NMRW), Aberystwyth, and the regional Sites and Monuments Record of the Clwyd-Powys Archaeological Trust, Welshpool. A copy of the Integrated Land Management Plan for the Sennybridge Training Area can be consulted at the NMRW, as well as at Defence Estates, Brecon Barracks (Tel: 01874 613881) and Powys County Council, Brecon (Tel: 01874 622141). The Disgwylfa visitor centre, picnic area and nature walk (with full disabled access) is well worth a visit and is located at map reference SN 993 438, at Pentre Dolau Honddu on the B4519 Garth to Upper Chapel road, north-west of Brecon.

THE ECONOMIC POTENTIAL OF THE UPLAND HERITAGE

John Wildig (ADAS)

Introduction

Our upland heritage arises from a process of continuous and continuing change. The story of Pwllpeiran, a mountain sheep unit in the upper Ystwyth Valley in Ceredigion, a place long associated with change and development in the uplands of Wales, is an exemplar of how new life can be injected into an ecologically degraded and economically depressed upland landscape.

In the upper Ystwyth Valley the hand of man has been superimposed upon a dramatic natural landscape at every vista. Archaeological and historical sites include prehistoric cairns and encampments on the hill tops, sites of old farmsteads, medieval roads and drovers' routes. Of particular note are the remains of former mining activities. The mining investment frenzy of the 1860s transformed the Ystwyth Valley into a veritable Klondike, with large communities of miners living, working and dying in the locality. The local mining industry has long gone and the landscape as we see it today has been restructured by the sheep and sitka monocultures created by government policies which were originally intended to sustain rural incomes and maintain populations.

However, today's intensive sheep farming is not a recent development. Large-scale sheep husbandry was introduced to the area by the Cistercians, whose agricultural granges encompassed large tracts of upland. After the Dissolution the monastic estates were taken over by a local aristocracy, before a *freehold revolution* allowed former tenants to acquire their own holdings (Davies, 1974). However, environmental and financial conditions were never very favourable, a situation exacerbated by successive agrarian crises. The isolation and toughness required to win a living from such inhospitable environments led to today's landscape of scattered hill farms,

Hill-walking and rambling are major activities in the Welsh uplands. Here a group of ramblers at Moel y Sych Bronze Age cairn in the Berwyns pauses to watch the aerial photographer overhead. 94-cs-0980

(opposite) The remains of derelict industrial landscapes in the uplands, whilst having great archaeological potential, are sometimes cleared away for new uses. This giant landscape sculpture of a horse forms the centrepiece of the Penallta Community Park in South Wales, on the site of the former spoil tips of the Penallta colliery. 99-cs-2113

Bryntail lead mine, near Llŷn Clywedog, Powys. An example of an industrial site in a rural setting, consolidated and presented for the public. 98-cs-0903

small market towns and afforestation, away from which there has been a long and continuing movement of the population in search of new employment opportunities.

In more recent times the problems of the upland areas of the United Kingdom have attracted the attention of government policy makers, who have seen as one of their objectives *the need to sustain rural incomes and populations*. Their response has been very much a top-down, production-orientated approach which, as already indicated, has seen the shape and structure of the uplands materially changed by increasing monocultures of sheep farming and sitka plantations.

The Story of Pwllpeiran

Pwllpeiran was formerly part of the estate of Thomas Johnes, whose vision and energy in the late eighteenth and early nineteenth centuries saw the famous Hafod Estate become a place of outstanding importance in the history of Picturesque Landscape and Aesthetics. In the 1930s Pwllpeiran again came to prominence as the headquarters of Sir George Stapledon's Cahn Hill Improvement Scheme. Stapledon's upland improvement work made Pwllpeiran world-famous, showcasing his profound ideas on the harmony between humankind and nature, a model for the sustainable development required for the future. From 1955 Pwllpeiran became a very successful Ministry of Agriculture, Fisheries and Food (MAFF) Experimental Husbandry Farm. As part of the government agricultural extension service it did much to encourage farmers in the uplands to re-seed pastures and feed and manage their stock for greater production at a time when increasing agricultural output was seen by policy makers as a way of maintaining rural populations and incomes. Today Pwllpeiran is part of ADAS, a leading private consultancy organisation to land-based industries in England and Wales, and is now the ADAS research centre for Wales. Its operating brief goes some way beyond production *per se*, appropriate at a time when environmental issues are of paramount importance and agriculture and forestry are at the mercy of global markets .

The Failure of Production-orientated Policies in the Uplands

The production-orientated policies of the 1970s, though successful in dramatically increasing production, led, through specialisation, to degraded landscapes and loss of biodiversity, and failed ultimately to maintain jobs and populations. From the mid-1990s the uplands have become increasingly managed for multiple objectives. As more sensitive agricultural and forestry systems came into vogue it became apparent that the restoration and subsequent management of habitats and ecosystems, which had been damaged by production-orientated agriculture and forestry, would be a major problem for land managers in the twenty-first century. In responding to these new challenges Pwllpeiran led an EU Objective 5b initiative, the Mynydd y Ffynnon Project, which recognised that agriculture and forestry needed to become more sustainable and that a broader approach to socio-economic development was required in the uplands. Mynydd y Ffynnon is now recognised as an innovative, pioneering, land-management project which brought together land users and conservation bodies in an attempt to tackle directly some of the many problems of the uplands. It has resulted in the restoration of habitats and ecosystems and the creation of new multipurpose woodlands and open spaces in forestry plantations. As part of this wider, more holistic, approach archaeology and heritage were brought into prominence through the undertaking of a comprehensive programme of intensive archaeological reconnaissance survey within the project area. This allowed the integration of archaeological

ADAS Pwllpeiran experimental farm, from the air. 2001-cs-374

data into land management and other initiatives arising from the project. However, as the project was drawing to a close it became apparent that rural communities needed to become involved, as much to maintain the upland landscape in an acceptable condition as to secure their own future. One of the outcomes of the project was the realisation that cultural landscape and biodiversity, once sacrificed without thought on

The Disgwylfa visitor centre on the Sennybridge Training Area (Mynydd Epynt), Powys. The restored farmhouse features displays and exhibitions, whilst there is an upland nature trail with full disabled access nearby. 2002-cs-4003

the altar of production, must now be regarded as *a primary resource* for the development of sustainable landscapes and cultural tourism.

More and more people are enjoying the countryside, the economic potential of which is only now beginning to be realised. In 1998 walking and mountaineering are estimated to have generated £77 million for the economy of rural Wales at a time when the economic fortunes of farming and forestry were steadily declining. Heritage and history, through adding value to the visitor experience, are vital ingredients in the mix of activities required for sustainable rural development.

How can Cultural Landscapes and Biodiversity be Used ?

Sustainable systems for agriculture and forestry are only part of the solution. Socio-economic development in the wider sense will be needed. Green tourism, focusing on the discerning, higher income visitor with an appetite for knowledge about landscape, history, heritage, agriculture and forestry, will become increasingly important. Environmental enhancement and socio-economic development will come from taking the best of the past and melding it with the appropriate technical, cultural and economic associations of the twenty-first century to create sustainable communities who will manage the countryside for the multiple objectives required in today's demanding world.

Pwllpeiran's Agritourism Project

To take this concept further Pwllpeiran secured funding for a second EU Objective 5b-funded initiative, the Pwllpeiran Agritourism Project. This has the following objectives:

- creating new access
- creating access to knowledge
- environmental-impact monitoring
- socio-economic monitoring
- dissemination of information and
- countryside management

The project, although seriously affected by the shut down of the countryside through the outbreak of foot-and-mouth disease in 2001, has been a tremendous success in that it has demonstrated again the value of a fully integrated approach to the management of the uplands and highlighted the way that knowledge can be utilised within the wider community.

Information Board at Pwllpeiran: the opening up of the countryside because of CROW legislation has focused attention on its intrinsic interest, especially the uplands with their attractions for ramblers. This provides opportunities to present the results of Uplands Initiative surveys to visitors in an entertaining and informative manner. The heritage information board shown here is one of several positioned along the Peiran Trail in a part of upland Ceredigion which lay in the Mynydd y Ffynnon survey area. C2002-035-04

The Pwllpeiran Trail

The cornerstone of the project has been the construction of the Pwllpeiran Trail, an exciting seven kilometre circular walk. The area round Pwllpeiran has magnificent scenery, but the key to setting up the trail was the co-operation and collaboration of *all* interested parties. One of the first priorities was to canvass the views of local ramblers who walked the proposed route. The Royal Commission on the Ancient and Historical Monuments of Wales was involved in discussions on how to draw out the historical potential of an area which forms part of a Landscape of Outstanding Historic Interest, containing a number of protected monuments including deserted rural settlements and early farmsteads. However, the trail could only become a factor in socio-economic development through being promoted and marketed. Attractive leaflets and information boards were devised, and

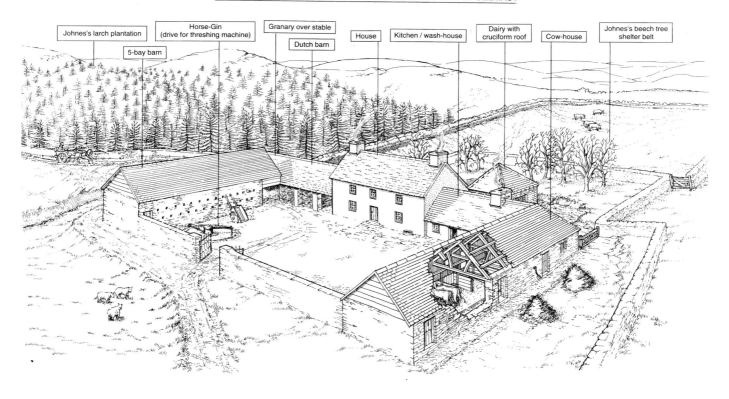

Johnes's larch plantation

5-bay barn

Horse-Gin (drive for threshing machine)

Granary over stable

Dutch barn

House

Kitchen / wash-house

Dairy with cruciform roof

Cow-house

Johnes's beech tree shelter belt

Reconstruction of Johnes's experimental farm at Gelmast, prepared for interpretation boards on the Peiran Trail. RCAHMW drawing

ADAS Pwllpeiran became increasingly involved with the local community, especially through Pentir Pumlumon, a group of local small tourism businesses seeking to develop and market this part of mid-Wales in a sustainable fashion.

From August 2001, as the countryside tried to return to normal following the foot-and-mouth outbreak, the trail has become very popular and acclaimed by both visitors and locals alike. By the end of the year five hundred people were recorded on the monitors as having used the trail.

In June 2002 the project came to an end, and as the evaluation of the data gets underway positive messages are emerging. There is a greater need than ever for a more broadly-based rural economy where, for example, farmers will be able to derive income from a range of different opportunities. The need to diversify will become increasingly important and attempts must be made to group opportunities together into marketable packages.

The Pwllpeiran Trail has been a very useful exemplar and stimulated interest amongst farmers in other localities, who are increasingly beginning to realise that more sensitive farming systems can benefit the environment, themselves and their communities through the potential of cultural heritage to create jobs and attract visitors to stay in the area.

Transposing this to the Wider Upland Scene

This section has as its title 'The Economic Potential of the Upland Heritage' and has focused especially on the story of Pwllpeiran. However, the experience gained here is applicable to the wider upland scene. Several actions are seen as being of paramount importance in this context if rural communities are to survive and the economic value of the upland heritage is to be realised. It is essential to utilise the opportunities of an area to the full, investigating partnerships for maximum benefits and looking ahead at all times, adapting as necessary to constantly changing market requirements. New visions are important for the future and should be developed to the full in a sustainable fashion.

Blaenafon Ironworks: the first purpose-built multi-furnace ironworks in the world (from 1788-9) undergoing consolidation. The raw-material needs of this works transformed the surrounding upland landscape, and its large on-going programme of consolidation is enhancing the appeal of one of the main tourist draws at the centre of this World Heritage Site. 1621820/3/0036

THE ECONOMICS OF CULTURAL LANDSCAPES

John Rodger (Torfaen County Borough Council)

The Blaenafon World Heritage Project is a unique and ambitious venture trying to achieve economic regeneration of an area through sympathetic exploitation of a cultural landscape. This historic landscape is now being used to attract visitors and act as a catalyst for the regeneration of the economically depressed community of Blaenafon.

The Blaenafon Industrial Landscape has been defined by UNESCO as a 'Cultural Landscape'. The many Scheduled Ancient Monuments and the town of Blaenafon itself are part of a great contextual landscape created during the formative years of the Industrial Revolution. The Industrial Landscape was inscribed as a World Heritage Site in December 2000. The World Heritage Committee agreed its outstanding international value:

'The area around Blaenafon bears eloquent and exceptional testimony to the pre-eminence of South Wales as the World's major producer of iron and coal in the 19th century. All the necessary elements can be seen in situ coal and ore mines, quarries, a primitive railway system, furnaces, the homes of the workers, and the social infrastructure of their community'. (ICOMOS 2000).

The Blaenafon World Heritage Site is a mountain-top landscape extending to some 33,000 hectares and falling from a height of 581 metres to 70 metres. Forty-five per cent of the landscape is within the Brecon Beacons National Park. Blaenafon is a 'cultural landscape' in which the 'combined works of nature and man' can be readily observed (UNESCO 1999). Much of the landscape is derelict, being the remains of early mineral exploitation. The landscape contains several very significant Scheduled Ancient Monuments, particularly the original Blaenafon Ironworks of 1789, Big Pit (now The National Mining Museum of Wales) and Hill's Tramroad, an early railway system which leads down to the Brecknock & Abergavenny Canal.

The achievement of World Heritage Site status is not seen by the Blaenafon Partnership simply as an end in itself. The stated main aim is:

'To protect and conserve this landscape so that future generations may understand the contribution South Wales made to the Industrial Revolution. By presentation and promotion of the Blaenafon Industrial Landscape it is intended to increase cultural tourism and assist the economic regeneration of the area'. (Blaenavon 1999).

The potential economic returns from the Blaenafon Industrial Landscape are very significant, but achieving the benefits requires the effective realisation of a matrix of projects based on the protection, conservation, presentation and promotion of the main features in the landscape.

This matrix approach was confirmed in a recent study by the Business School of Cardiff University into the economic impact of the Blaenafon Project. The study concluded that a positive economic impact is possible through the sensitive exploitation of Blaenafon's unique industrial landscape. However, to capture the benefits requires the realisation simultaneously of a number of complementary projects to achieve an effective critical mass. The Blaenafon Project is still in the early formative years as the conditions for effective regeneration are being put systematically in place.

World Heritage Site status has altered perceptions of the area, previously regarded as not only to be lacking in interest but actually needing to be cleared as derelict land. From the increasingly positive perception of the area cultural tourism has begun to grow and flourish.

The visitor/educational potential of key monuments is being developed. The previously fragile future of Big Pit has been secured, and since February 2001 it has been owned and managed by the National Museums and Galleries of Wales (NMGW) as the National Mining Museum for Wales. The complex is presently being repaired, restored and re-branded at a cost of £7 million, with the aid of a Heritage Lottery Grant of more than £5 million. Visitor numbers increased from 77,000 to 120,000 due largely to the free entry policy of NMGW.

The Blaenafon Ironworks of 1789, the focus of the World Heritage Site, is now being developed to encourage visitors through continuing restoration of the structures on site and improved presentation to visitors. A Tourist Information Centre has been opened on site, which assists in marketing the area and co-ordinating educational site visits. Visitor numbers have doubled from 4,284 to 7,212 in the year following the inscription of Blaenafon as a World Heritage Site.

The potential to extend the limited options of the Pontypool and Blaenafon Railway Company from a track length of 1 kilometre to 3.5 kilometres in the short term, and then 10 kilometres in the longer term, is being explored. It is considered that the 'steam railway experience' complements

Hill's Tramroad Walk: walkers exploring one of several tunnels on the hillside terrace tracks that were built as a system of early railways (1818), including one underground section that was the largest in the world at the time. These are being conserved as part of a system of pedestrian and cycle ways to provide and improve access into the World Heritage Site. 080302V2J218313

the on-site experiences at the Ironworks, Big Pit, and other heritage features in the town. Visitor figures for the railway also increased from 6,878 to 8,701.

The Brecknock & Abergavenny Canal has two wharves within the World Heritage Site, and the growing economic value of the canal for pleasure cruising can link with visits to other parts of the World Heritage Site. Just outside the World Heritage Site boundary, Goytre Wharf has been developed as a visitor centre and provides an important gateway to the World Heritage Site. In the first year of operation the new centre attracted many extra visitors.

In the town of Blaenafon the historic St Peter's School complex (*c.*1815) is about to be restored as a World Heritage Site Centre. The former school buildings will provide a stand alone attraction with interactive media, digital archive and facilities for students of all ages. The centre will host exhibitions and an events programme. This will mean that it is continually renewing its offer as a visitor attraction. It is anticipated that the National Trust will play a key role in the centre, and there will be direct community involvement. The St Peter's centre will attract at least 15,000 people annually, which will greatly benefit the town centre.

The town centre retail area is currently in a run-down condition with several empty and boarded-up shops. This is now the subject of proposals to bring shops back into effective use; a substantial art and crafts component will probably be included. The fabric of the town centre housing is being progressively restored with the benefit of Neighbourhood Renewal Area grants worth £15 million over ten years provided by the Welsh Assembly Government. This programme is making properties more attractive and reversing the spiral of decline in house prices. Although this is basically a housing repair programme it is proving to be of considerable conservation value.

The broken but interesting landscape of mineral exploitation also provides opportunities for cyclists, walkers, cavers, and hang-gliding enthusiasts. A £1 million rolling programme of access improvement and interpretation is now being developed. In particular it is intended to provide local loops within the WHS from the SUSTRANS national cycle trail which runs through the landscape. Defined walks identified in leaflets and interpreted by well designed display panels at key sites are in the process of being developed. This work in the landscape will need to be carried out in close liaison with landowners and commoners as most of the landscape is 'Urban Common'.

There is potential to attract visitors to the town from the various established attractions in the landscape. As visitor numbers rise changes for the better in the economy of the town can be attributed to the historic landscape. A very important aspect of the promotion of the industrial landscape is linking to the much visited outstanding natural landscape of the Brecon Beacons National Park and the well known attractions of rural Monmouthshire with its market towns, particularly nearby Abergavenny (Y Fenni). The opportunity to link the traditional rural areas of mid-Wales with the less well known industrial heritage areas of South Wales is something the Blaenafon Partnership is determined to achieve.

Conclusions

Since 1997 the concept of achieving regeneration through heritage at Blaenafon has been vigorously pursued by the Blaenafon Partnership. It is the partnership ideal that can serve as a model for other broadly-based and strongly supported initiatives in the uplands. At Blaenafon the partnership consists of Torfaen County Borough Council; Monmouthshire County Council; Blaenau Gwent County Borough Council; Brecon Beacons National Park; Cadw: Welsh Historic Monuments; The Royal Commission on the Ancient and Historical Monuments of Wales; the National Museums and Galleries of Wales; the Countryside Council for Wales; the Wales Tourist Board; the Welsh Development Agency; British Waterways; and the National Trust. The attainment of World Heritage Site status in December 2000 put Blaenafon on the world map and provided the catalyst for economic recovery.

Schemes have been developed over the last four years for the protection, conservation, presentation and promotion of the World Heritage Site, which will exceed £25 million by 2005. There have already been tangible benefits to the community of Blaenafon from the World Heritage Site status of the Blaenafon Industrial Landscape. World Heritage Site status has helped secure and create jobs, has encouraged investment, increased visitor numbers, and changed the perception of the town. It has resulted in the reversal of the downward trend in property values and a raising in investment levels. However, we are only at the beginning of a long haul. Much clearly remains to be done.

Barbara Lewis, chairman of the Blaenafon Traders Association, has stated that: *"Everything is moving at last. We know it's going to be a long slow process but there has been a huge difference already"*. The expectation is that over a ten- to twenty-year period the Blaenafon Industrial Landscape will achieve similar change and betterment to that enjoyed by the Ironbridge Gorge in Shropshire following its World Heritage Site inscription in 1986.

Llanfoist Canal Wharf: the Brecknock & Abergavenny Canal runs along the upland fringe of the Blaenafon World Heritage Site and is already a significant generator of income with its growing pleasure-cruising use. The rich heritage of buildings alongside the canal includes several of the earliest railway warehouses in the world (dating from 1819-21), which stored finished iron and other valuable goods. CS-95-IAB-57

Blaenafon Town: these houses on Park Street were part of the eighteenth- and nineteenth-century upland hillside settlement developed by the Blaenavon Iron & Coal Company and its workforce. The town's population has halved since the nineteenth-century zenith of the ironworks, but conservation and sympathetic improvement of the housing stock is now underway. V2J/8126/17D NPRN304562

Llidiartywaun Windfarm, Powys: the Welsh uplands have proved to be ideal locations for wind turbine developments. Government initiatives intended to meet the Non-Fossil Fuel Obligation will undoubtedly result in the construction of more. The need to develop renewable energy resources must be balanced against the intrusive physical and visual impact such developments can have on otherwise little developed landscapes. 2001-cs-1637

SITE PRESERVATION AND MANAGEMENT

Kathryn Roberts (Cadw) and Paul Sambrook (Cambria Archaeology)

Introduction

One of the many outcomes of the Uplands Initiative surveys has been the provision of information for historic landscape management. In order to develop protection strategies for the historic environment first and foremost there is a need for good information. The numbers of new sites identified during the Uplands Initiative surveys, along with the extensive enhancement of older records, have provided a greater understanding of the upland landscapes of Wales and formed a basis for the development of future investigative and protection strategies.

Within the present context of a changing rural economy there are opportunities for different forms of uplands exploitation. These include large-scale alternative energy developments, forestry and agricultural 'land improvement', as well as smaller-scale usage such as increased tourism and recreational activities. It is not intended to reiterate here the effects such land uses can have on the historic environment since others have already done so (Darvill 1987; Darvill and Fulton 1998), but to consider some of the means by which their long-term impacts can be managed within a Welsh context.

As information was collected during the Uplands Initiative surveys it was immediately put to work by the heritage management organisations operating in Wales. The data, as maintained in the National Monuments Record of Wales (managed by the RCAHMW) and the four regional Sites and Monuments Records (managed by the Welsh Archaeological Trusts), are used for provision of management advice and recommendations, as well as the formulation of longer term protection policies.

The updated records form the basis for general and specific advice on the potential impact on the historic environment of development proposals. They also provide information and management advice on the historic features to be found on their land to landowners applying to enter agri-environment schemes such as *Tir Gofal* (Countryside Council for Wales 1998).

In addition, the results of the Uplands Initiative surveys have helped to form the working databases for several Cadw: Welsh Historic Monuments pan-Wales monument protection programmes, including the Scheduling Enhancement and Threat-Related Surveys of deserted rural settlements (Cadw forthcoming) and prehistoric funerary and ritual monuments.

Gwersyll ringwork and cairns, Glamorgan: buried in a dense coniferous plantation are a semi-circular ringwork and burial cairns at Gwersyll, Glamorgan. Although not particularly accessible the features have been protected within the open forest glade. Today many plantations like this are reaching maturity and being felled, bringing new threats to archaeological sites within them. Maintaining archaeological monuments in open areas can be labour-intensive and will not necessarily be appropriate for all sites. 99-cs-1637

These surveys differ from those of the Uplands Initiative in that their aim is to provide specific assessments of monument condition for management purposes. Since they are based on the contents of the Sites and Monument Records they both benefit from and build upon the enhanced survey records produced by the Uplands Initiative.

Enclosures at Nant Tarthwynni, Brecknock: two Iron Age enclosures demonstrate the effects of different upland land-use: forest (left of picture) and open moor (right of picture). This view taken ten years ago shows them before the densely planted forest matured. Today the enclosures are completely obscured and their condition is difficult to assess. 90-cs-412

Preservation and pressures

The publication *Ancient Monuments in the Countryside* (Darvill 1987) recognised the archaeological importance of upland areas and summarised the principal threats facing them. Although written with reference to England much of its discussion was equally applicable to Wales at that time, and continues to be so today. In general the uplands have been spared the effects of the single greatest threat to archaeological monument preservation – intensive arable agriculture. Yet they are still vulnerable to intensification of other traditional land-use practices – land improvement, grazing, military use and mineral exploitation. Alongside these, and often connected with them, are the effects of erosion, both natural and by humans, which could well become an even greater threat in the future when public access increases (Countryside and Rights of Way Act 2000).

To these threats can be added forestry and large-scale alternative energy developments. Approximately 14 per cent of Wales is under woodland cover, with two-thirds being non-native conifers, particularly common in upland areas (National Assembly for Wales, 2001). Many of the forests planted in the early post-war years are now reaching maturity and are being felled and replanted. This renewed activity can threaten

surviving archaeological monuments but also offers new opportunities for archaeological investigation (see Mynydd y Ffynnon case study). The Government drive to meet the Non-Fossil Fuel Obligation (NFFO) introduced following the Electricity Act 1989 has led to the construction of fourteen wind turbine power stations in Wales, many in the uplands (about 49 per cent of the UK total), and more are in the planning stage (Countryside Council for Wales 1999).

Mechanisms for Protection

Perhaps the most direct form of monument protection is the process of scheduling. On behalf of the National Assembly for Wales, Cadw: Welsh Historic Monuments compiles and maintains a 'schedule' of monuments of national importance. These 'Scheduled Ancient Monuments', or SAMs, enjoy statutory protection under the *Ancient Monuments and Archaeological Areas Act 1979*. It is worth noting that, to date, over thirty-five sites have been added to the 'schedule' as a direct result of the Uplands Initiative, with more sites added through subsequent survey programmes.

Since scheduling can only be applied to monuments considered of national importance, these numbers reflect both the well-preserved state of many upland monuments and the

Tal-y-garreg Hillfort, Gwynedd: the physical defences that once protected Tal-y-garreg Iron Age hillfort would offer little defence against the threat of industrial-scale extraction. Quarrying has extended to the very edge of the monument, isolating it from other contemporary sites and altering its setting beyond recognition. Although the fort is protected as a Scheduled Ancient Monument this has not prevented the destruction of surrounding features. Bronze Age halberds discovered within the quarry hint at a prehistoric landscape of which much has now been lost. 95-cs-2252

previous lack of fieldwork. There are, however, limitations on the extent to which scheduling can be applied in the uplands. Scheduling is best suited to protecting individual monuments and definable, limited areas rather than extensive landscapes. While it can be beneficial in drawing the attention of both landowners and users to the key historic elements in the landscape, it does not necessarily prevent changes from occurring which may result in their isolation from other contemporary features.

Intended to help redress this problem is the Register of Landscapes of Historic Interest in Wales produced as a joint exercise by Cadw: Welsh Historic Monuments, the Countryside Council for Wales and ICOMOS, UK (Cadw: Welsh Historic Monuments 1998 and 2001). Wales has the

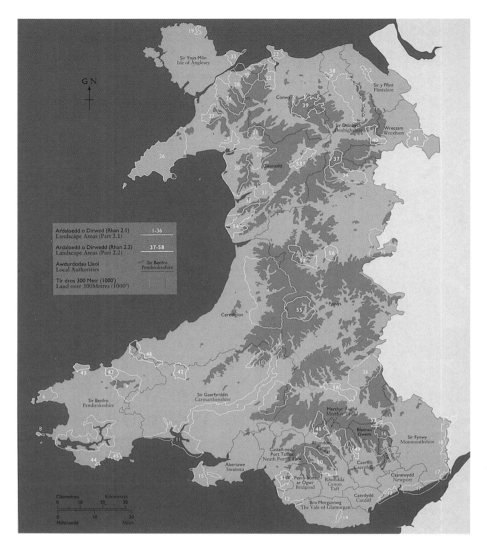

The uplands are of national importance. This map shows the regions which feature in the Registers of Landscapes of Outstanding and Special Historic Interest in Wales. Many either lie within, or include parts of, upland areas. Numbers refer to the listings in the registers.

distinction of being the first nation in Europe to have compiled such a register, which provides holistic descriptions of fifty-eight landscapes of distinctive character. The Register, which is non-statutory (landscapes are not designated), provides authoritative information that can be used by a whole range of organisations, at both national and local levels, and by landowners, farmers and all those with an interest in the Welsh landscape. It is taken into account when unitary development plans are being prepared and when considering the implications of developments which are of such a scale that they would have a more than local impact on an area on the Register. Amongst the fifty-eight registered landscapes are several upland regions including the Blaenafon World Heritage Site, the Vale of Clwyd, upland Ceredigion (including Mynydd y Ffynnon), Holywell Common, the Denbigh Moors and the Berwyns.

Given the different pressures upon them it is clear that management of the diverse archaeological remains of the uplands requires a different approach from those of the lowlands. Many of the legal mechanisms which have been developed during the past century for the protection of archaeological monuments are of only limited value in the uplands. This is most evident with regard to the planning process (Welsh Assembly Government 2002). While this can mitigate the impacts of large-scale developments such as windfarms, water-power schemes and extractive industries (all of which require environmental impact assessments), it is less effective against the creeping effects of agricultural improvement (which do not).

Moel y Gaer, Denbighshire: the effects of erosion by visitors are clearly visible as the thin soil covering the hillfort interior is worn away. Cases like this may require positive intervention in the form of conservation repairs, protective mats or sacrificial surfaces in order to limit ongoing damage to the monument. Fortunately the presence of thick undergrowth limits the damage to the paths crossing the hillfort interior, unlike the case of nearby Moel y Gamelin where nearly the entire cairn has been affected by this sort of erosion. 935510-2; 2001-cs-0909

Developing long-term management strategies

To develop and achieve successful protection strategies requires accessible and accurate information (available from the National Monuments Record of Wales and the regional Sites and Monuments Records), sympathetic landowners willing to adapt their methods in order to mitigate against damage and, finally, a means of combining the two. Perhaps the greatest difficulty that has faced archaeologists in the past has been a failure properly to communicate with those best placed to offer practical assistance.

These include: landowners (both organisations and individuals), together with developers; Unitary Authorities (through their development plans, countryside strategies, warden services, economic development strategies, biodiversity action plans, access and leisure strategies); local communities; preservation groups and organisations; Forestry Commission (through Woodland Grant Schemes and Forest Design Strategies); the Countryside Council for Wales; and the Environment Agency (Thompson and Yates 1999). Fortunately, the opportunities for such contacts are good and improving, with the Royal Commission and the Welsh Archaeological Trusts particularly active in seeking wider recognition of the historic environment.

There is clearly growing support for sustainable development strategies, as demonstrated by schemes such as the Forest Enterprise Welsh Heritage Assets Survey and the All-Wales Agri-Environment Scheme, *Tir Gofal* (Countryside Council for Wales, 1998), both of which offer practical opportunities and mechanisms for heritage management. These schemes are considered in more detail within the context of the Mynydd y Ffynnon Survey (see below).

The essential requirements for any strategy are information and communication, particularly when it is remembered that actions intended to preserve one resource are not necessarily appropriate for another. For example, although the needs of wildlife and heritage protection can be complementary this is not always the case, as evidenced in the Berwyn SSSI where re-introduction of heather was preceded by ground scarification.

An example where positive management strategies have been implemented within an upland landscape is at Mynydd y Ffynnon, Ceredigion.

Management in action : Mynydd y Ffynnon

The archaeological survey of this important area has already been discussed by Paul Sambrook elsewhere in this volume . The land lies in the ownership of three main interests: Forest Enterprise, the Agricultural Development and Advisory Service (ADAS), (both of which part-funded the survey), and a number of individual private landowners. The Mynydd y Ffynnon project was in progress between 1996 and 2001 and

113

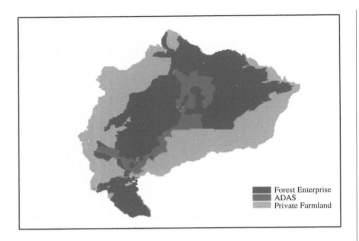

Map showing land in the Mynydd y ffynnon project area in the ownership of ADAS and Forest Enterprise, and land in private ownership.

Forest Enterprise
ADAS
Private Farmland

included eight separate phases of work, most of which included elements of fieldwork and/or desktop research.

The survey initially developed following a ground-breaking initiative undertaken by Forest Enterprise Wales intended to produce an inventory of all the archaeological sites on their land holdings throughout Wales. The project, known as the Welsh Historic Assets (WHA) Survey, was initiated during the mid-1990s as a response to the changing economic climate and increased environmental awareness affecting forestry. The large-scale afforestation strategies of the twentieth century are no longer supported. As the coniferous plantations of the 1950s come to maturity and are felled they are being replaced with open landscapes and less intensively planted native hardwoods, which offer more benefits than solely economic ones. The recognition of archaeological sites as 'assets' has enabled plans to be developed which provide for their long-term protection.

The project was intended to provide up-to-date records for a new Forest Enterprise database (DOLMEN). Project fieldworkers were asked to provide both physical information and detailed management recommendations for each archaeological site that would become an integral element in future Forest Enterprise management processes, including future forest development plans. A typical management recommendation would include specific suggestions intended to improve the condition of a particular site, such as reducing tree cover, creating access routes to sites and opening links between monuments.

The second major landowner in the Mynydd y Ffynnon area is ADAS, which operates an experimental farm at Pwllpeiran, discussed elsewhere in this book. Close liaison between Forest Enterprise and ADAS led to a similar survey being commissioned for their land holding in order to provide the same depth of information and to produce individual site management recommendations. Due to their engagement in experimental investigations into the effects of different farming methods, ADAS are ideally placed to consider the impacts of different strategies on monument survival.

Private farmland within the survey area is in the ownership of several families, each of which has its own management regime. Survey of this land was funded by RCAHMW under the auspices of the Uplands Initiative. Being a reconnaissance and site recording exercise this survey did not include the provision of individual site management prescriptions, though some sites were recommended (and subsequently selected) for statutory protection. In consequence, contact between these landowners and archaeologists was more limited than was the case for ADAS and Forest Enterprise, although continued contact through the Cadw monitoring programme is assured where monuments have been scheduled. Although specific management recommendations were not produced the information gathered during the survey could be utilised for this purpose and could form the basis of future management plans should any of the farms choose to enter into schemes such as *Tir Gofal*.

The development of agri-environmental farming schemes has enormous potential (albeit only partially fulfilled at present) towards positive management of sites and historic landscapes. The recognition of archaeological features on a farm as one of the qualifying measures for acceptance in the *Tir Gofal* scheme places the historic environment on the same footing as other environmental and wildlife concerns. However, there is always room for improvement. At present archaeologists visit only 20 per cent of farms joining the scheme, and although management recommendations are made by archaeologists it is *Tir Gofal* project officers who draw up the final management plans. The scheme has, however, led to positive benefits being felt in many areas.

Conclusion

In effect a safety net has been created in respect of all known archaeological and historic sites within the Mynydd y Ffynnon survey area. This takes the form of the site records and project

Partly reclaimed industrial landscape, Dowlais, Merthyr Tydfil: an industrial landscape in transformation. The land that was once marked by mines, pits, slag heaps and other signs of an industrial past is being reclaimed and reshaped. The mining activities that swept away evidence for earlier land-use are in turn being removed from the landscape. 92-cs-1132

archives that now exist within the Sites and Monuments Records of Cambria Archaeology and the Clwyd-Powys Archaeological Trust, and in the National Monuments Record of Wales. Also included are the twenty Scheduled Ancient Monuments within the Mynydd y Ffynnon survey area (the best of the known archaeology of the district), which have been given statutory protection by Cadw.

If there is a single message to come from this initiative it is the benefit of good communication between archaeologists, landowners and land managers. Protection requires co-operation based on sound information, both of individual sites and wider historic landscapes.

Management of the historic environment must be pragmatic. Upland landscapes are dynamic; they are living products of change and reflect the way developing societies adapt to new circumstances. The objective therefore is to ensure the sympathetic preservation of evidence of previous generations without stifling modern innovation and use.

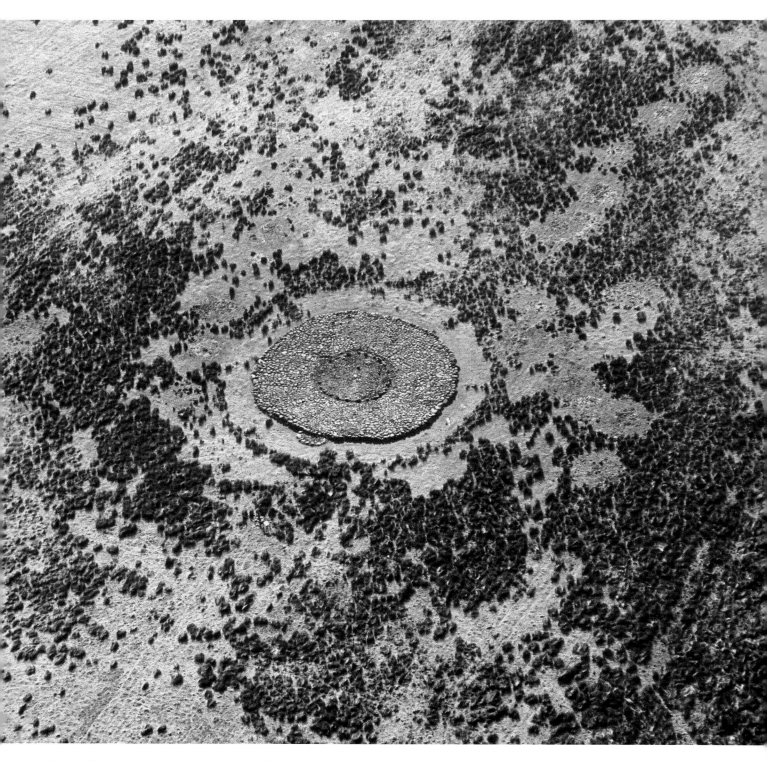

Brenig Cairn: the reconstructed stone-rubble circle of platform cairn 51 is one of a number of sites excavated during the construction of the Brenig Reservoir and since made readily accessible to visitors and tourists as part of the Brenig Archaeological Trail near Denbigh. 91-cs-117

THE ACHIEVEMENTS AND FUTURE OF THE UPLANDS INITIATIVE

Stephen Hughes (Royal Commission on the Ancient and Historical Monuments of Wales)

The Achievements of the Initiative

When the Uplands Initiative was first mooted in 1989 most of the known uplands archaeology dated from the prehistoric and Roman periods. There has been a long antiquarian tradition of searching for and identifying prehistoric sites, and many occupy visually prominent locations such as ridges and hilltops. As a result it was expected that the initiative might greatly increase the number of sites of those early periods. In fact, the increase was negligible for most sites in this period, and indeed this focused reappraisal actually reduced the number of sites attributed to the Roman period (Sambrook *et al.* 1999, 29). In the North Radnorshire Commons Uplands Survey, for example, no less than thirteen prehistoric cairns and barrows were already on the record out of a known total of twenty, and the survey produced only one further example (Hankinson 1999). The exception to the small increase in sites of this period in south-west Wales was a large (673 per cent) increase in the hitherto very small number of general early prehistoric sites, so that these two hundred and one sites now form 4.5 per cent of the total number of sites. There was also a significant increase in the number of Bronze Age monuments, as the great number and easily recognisable nature of burial cairns and burnt mounds ensured an increase of no less than 51 per cent in this type of monument in the uplands between 1989 and 1999; there are now one thousand and twenty-nine of these known, representing 22 per cent of all types of sites (Sambrook *et al.* 1999, 31). In the uplands archaeology surveys of mid- and east Wales whole new cairnfields have been identified in less prominent locations: seven near Cwmystwyth in mid Wales (PRN 38341: Silvester 1997a, 5.2), and on the Denbigh Moors in north-eastern Wales, where twenty burial or clearance cairns were identified (PRN 105708: Hankinson 1995b; Silvester 1999, 9).

It is sites of the medieval and later periods that have seen the greatest increases in new discoveries resulting from the Uplands Initiative. Throughout Wales these fall into two broad categories: structures related to seasonal settlement; and mines and quarries resulting from mineral exploitation. Overall figures for south-west Wales have been quantified to show an increase for sites of these periods of 125 per cent, to a total of 2672 sites, that is nearly 60 per cent of all the uplands sites recorded (Sambrook *et al.* 1999, 29).

Over most of upland Wales (almost half of the total area of the country) the number of archaeological sites of all periods discovered within the areas searched has increased eleven-fold.

The initiative has also illuminated the nature of two large areas of Wales where the upland landscapes of two very different eras are undoubtedly of international importance.

The uplands of north-west Wales arguably retain some of the best-preserved prehistoric landscapes in western Europe. This may be because of the abundance of surface stone in the area available to build field boundaries and other structures, whereas the use of wood leaves few superficial traces after its decay. A substantial amount of upland fieldwork carried out in eastern Wales led to the discovery of only one similar example, and significantly that lay in an area of land which formed the eastern extremity of the former county of Meirionnydd in east Wales (Silvester 1996).

Complex concentrations of industrial remains have also been located. An outstanding example is the landscape of Blaenafon in south-east Wales, now designated as a World Heritage Site. Here survey on the fossilised moorland landscape surrounding what were then the largest ironworks in the world has revealed an unexpected sophistication of water-power generation channels and early horse-drawn railway formations. These findings and their presentation to the world heritage assessor helped to facilitate the designation of this upland industrial landscape as an area of international importance. The interpretation of this World Heritage Site now presents part of the Welsh uplands to the rest of the international community.

Some of the individual components of this landscape are of international importance. Survey has shown that 'hushing'– the use of water released from dam sluices to remove soil overlying valuable mineral deposits – was much more widely applied than previously thought. The use of water power in driving the world's largest ironworks has left very extensive remains and belies the widely held assumption that the first industrial revolution was based on steam power alone. Early railways were evolving in south Wales at a crucial time of experiment in the development of the modern railway. More railways were built in south Wales during this period of experimentation with new types of track and locomotion than anywhere else at the end of the eighteenth and into the first three decades of the nineteenth centuries.

The uplands surveys have also clearly revealed the extent to which archaeology differs between the regions of Wales. One of the two most common types of sites in the uplands of north-west Wales is prehistoric hut circles (Thompson, D. 2000, 33). However, they hardly exist in other areas of Wales, although there seems to be no apparent reason for a lack of a substantial prehistoric population elsewhere. The answer may lie in the type of available raw materials. Stone is abundant in north-west Wales, as evidenced by the survival of complete relict stone-walled Iron Age field systems there, so that stone-built hut circles can easily be recognised for what they are. In east and south Wales such structures may have been constructed in timber, and as this has long decayed the only evidence may be so slight as to be unrecognisable or survive only as slight earthworks, or scoops, on the hillside. The type of hut settlement in the uplands varies from that found in the richer lands below. Scattered hut groups characterise lands between 300-400 metres, while nucleated enclosed hut groups are mostly found at 100-200 metres; single huts are most often found on the upland fringe between 200-300 metres and may reflect the demands of upland transhumance (Thompson, D. 2000, 21).

The initiative has revealed the existence of site types barely recognised before and existing in unexpectedly large numbers. The issue of statutory protection of selected examples has been addressed. It was recognised that there was a need to evaluate whole categories of monument. Accordingly, a series of thematic projects, sponsored by Cadw: Welsh Historic Monuments, has been carried-out on the most common categories of monument identified under the Uplands Initiative. The main types of monument examined have been long-huts and their ancillary structures in 'deserted rural settlements'; non-ferrous metals mines, the first study of which, in Ceredigion, was undertaken as part of the Uplands Initiative; and 'hut circles' or round huts.

The Future of the Initiative

The Uplands Initiative was started in 1989 in response to a widespread and ongoing programme of afforestation and extensive land improvement. Both these threats have receded. The most threatened upland landscapes are now those in the *Blaenau*, or Heads of the Valleys region, of south Wales where large-scale land reclamation and opencast mining, sometimes in combination, are in danger of destroying the whole of the landscape produced by the world's largest ironworks. The only exceptions that survive may be the World Heritage Site at Blaenafon and a few other protected areas. This makes survey of these areas a high priority.

The remoteness of the more rural upland areas of mid and north Wales may soon change as 'Right to Roam' (CROW) legislation is implemented over the next few years allowing access to huge areas of unenclosed upland. For this reason the Uplands Initiative has been redirected at these areas as a priority: the marginal and untouched nature of such land considered for survey is now regarded as being more important than any strict contour limit, although survey will mostly concern land over 200 metres. The drop in farm earnings means that rural areas will be more reliant on other sources of income such as tourism and that the known archaeological heritage of the uplands, with its largely intact historical landscape, is a major asset to be realised. There may well be some tourist erosion of key sites as the number of visitors increases, and it is important to locate significant archaeological features in order to safeguard and conserve them before this happens. This work complements the *Tir Gofal* farmland stewardship scheme which seeks to conserve and identify archaeological and traditional architectural features on mostly enclosed land. The Royal Commission on the Ancient and Historical Monuments of Wales, the Welsh Archaeological Trusts and Cadw: Welsh Historic Monuments are all associated with this scheme.

The Uplands Initiative began as a rapid reconnaissance project with the primary objectives of fixing the location of sites and compiling short database entries. A parallel reconnaissance programme has commenced through mapping the historic landscape from the huge resource of aerial photographs available in the National Monuments Record of Wales in Aberystwyth. This twin approach serves three purposes. First, it allows fieldworkers to locate on the ground features shown on aerial photographs. Second, it provides a wider landscape context for fieldworkers conducting ground surveys by traversing parallel lines across the landscape some 30 to 50 metres apart. Third, extensive patterns and networks of linear features such as field boundaries, watercourses and early horse-worked railways can only be effectively recorded, interpreted and understood by the use of aerial mapping. Conversely, there are issues that can only be resolved by field examination. Those carrying out the aerial mapping do not have a clear idea of the ground terrain or the extent to which

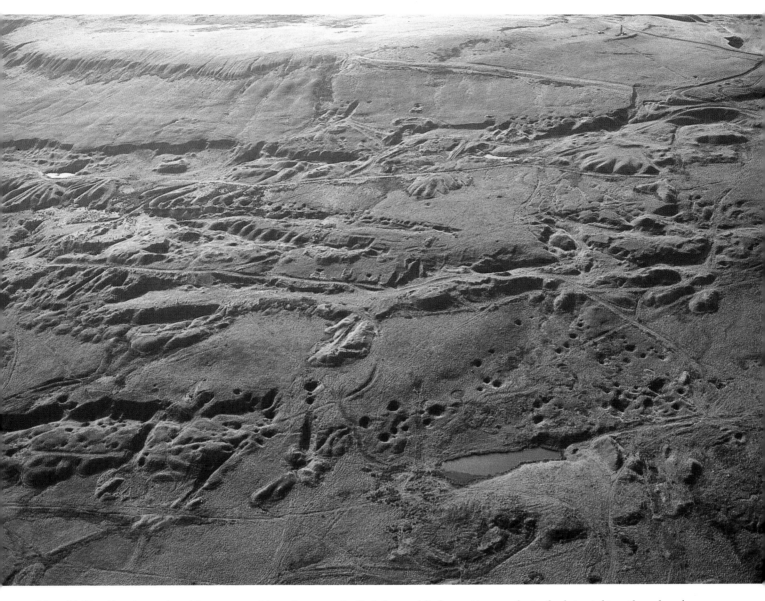

Mynydd Aberdâr: the coal and iron-ore workings that once fuelled the world's largest ironworks in the late eighteenth and early nineteenth centuries are a particularly vulnerable and increasingly rare type of upland landscape found on the present urban fringe. The very well preserved remains illustrated at Mynydd Aberdâr fed the Cyfarthfa Ironworks at Merthyr Tydfil (Tudful), and the four lines of workings across the picture (from the top) follow the outcropping of the nine feet seam, the middle coal measures, the lower coal measures and the Garw vein in the lower coal measures. 92-cs-0990

lighting at the time of photography may have distorted features being mapped. Archaeological and other sites appearing fresh in photographs of the 1940s may have been destroyed or at least have become considerably degraded. Furthermore, linear features such as those described can seem indistinguishable from the air but possess clear diagnostic features when viewed at ground level.

If a deeper understanding of the remains being discovered in the uplands is to be achieved it is essential that a more detailed examination of sites be carried out using appropriate techniques. Principal amongst these are techniques of excavation and palaeoecology, and their application to the Uplands Initiative will necessitate forming partnerships with practitioners. Excavation of upland Mesolithic hunter-gatherer sites together with the examination of fossil remains can provide invaluable evidence of the contemporary environment (Caseldine 2002). An upland dwelling represented only by rectangular foundations could potentially be a medieval *hafod* or summer dwelling associated with transhumance, a peat-cutter's or shepherd's shelter, or a nineteenth-century lead-miner's cottage. Many upland mining features are of uncertain date, and some could be very early. Open pits, trenches along mineral veins, prospecting trenches, multiple shaft mounds, water-hushing reservoirs and channels could conceivably date from the Bronze Age to the nineteenth century. Only more detailed examination will provide answers.

The Uplands Initiative has been largely concerned with extensive rapid survey, which has for the first time revealed what the most common monument types are in the uplands, but not provided a lot of information about the context and use of these structures. For that greater understanding there is a need for more archaeological excavation and palaeoenvironmental work.

The uplands surveys have also identified the location of the large areas of the uplands covered by peat. The recovery of pollen cores from these substantially undisturbed areas can yield invaluable information on the past natural history of the uplands. This is especially invaluable for the study of early man, and there is already evidence that early humans were altering their environment (Simmons 1996). In this Mesolithic period, or Middle Stone Age (*c.*8500-4200 BC), there is a need to focus on sites that have assemblages of flint tools and weapons. The availability of pollen and charcoal from associated sediments provides an opportunity for radiocarbon dates to be obtained which can establish a solid time-frame for the evidence of contemporary vegetation and its clearance with fires started by humans, or not, as the case may be.

In the Neolithic, or New Stone Age (*c.*4200-2000 BC), much of the available pollen evidence has been drawn from the uplands, and there is already an intention to correlate it as part of the Uplands Initiative. Much of the earliest farming took place in the lowlands, and there is a need to establish and clarify the contrasting forms of human activity between upland and lowland. An examination of palaeoenvironmental evidence is necessary to establish the nature of any seasonal occupation of the uplands in that early period (Caseldine 2003).

For the Bronze Age (*c.*2000-700 BC) Uplands Initiative surveys have added to the already large number of ceremonial and burial monuments, and the pollen record confirms that their appearance was accompanied by intensified clearance of woodland and shrub (Chambers 1982a; 1982b; 1983a; 1983b; and Smith and Cloutman 1988). The possible role of transhumance needs exploring in an economy where lowland cereal growing was developing but which was predominantly pastoral, even on the lowlands. Scientific studies could increase our understanding of the many uplands cairns sited on strategic hill crests dominating the skyline of the lowlands (Caseldine 2002). They could also elucidate the growing perception of the substantial Bronze Age mining activity that took place in the Welsh uplands, which has been demonstrated at Copa Hill, Cwmystwyth, by both radiocarbon and tree-ring dating of early timber water troughs (Mighall and Chambers 2003).

For the Iron Age (*c.*700 BC - AD 77) the pollen evidence for further clearance of the Uplands is uneven, and more systematic work needs to be done in this area. The acid soil of the uplands also means that the more traditional sources of evidence from archaeological finds is largely unobtainable as bone, pottery and metalwork seldom survive, a significant deficiency given the numbers of hillforts which survive in the uplands (Caseldine 2003).

In the Roman period (*c.*AD 77 - 410) there is a continued variation in clearance and woodland regeneration, which needs further regional pollen sampling and investigation. Romano-British society in the sub-Roman period is likely to have continued in some form in Wales for hundreds of years, but there are few pollen records for the period compared to the prehistoric sampling, and much further work needs to be done. The evidence for the sub-Roman and Early Medieval periods is very limited, but in the period *c.*AD 410-800 there is evidence of reduced activity in the uplands (Dark 2000, Fig. 5.6), contrasting with a continuity of land-use together with some increased activity in the lowlands (Caseldine 2003). Further work could investigate whether this is a consistent picture across the uplands.

In the Medieval and Post-medieval periods the nature and extent of transhumance, with cattle, stock and people moving between the lowland *hendre* farmstead and the attached upland *hafod* or *lluest* summer holding, should be investigated using palaeoenvironmental techniques. More evidence for possible uplands abandonment and resettlement due to climate changes and disease epidemics will be forthcoming from such work (Caseldine 2003; Bell and Dark 1997). Samples from upland bogs may also allow a quantification of non-ferrous-

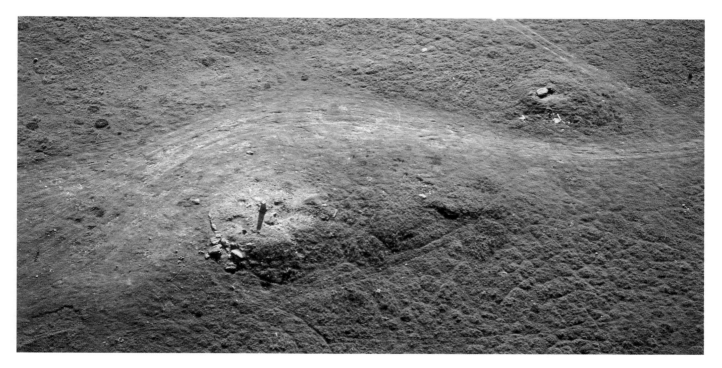

Carn Bugail Bronze Age Cairn: clearly visible curving round the cairn are the effects of visitor erosion from the many walkers attracted to Gelligaer Common in Mid Glamorgan: the erosion has helped expose the cairn kerb of two courses of flat-laid stones. The mountaintop cairn is itself disfigured by an Ordnance Survey triangulation marker positioned at its centre and standing on a damaged burial cist. The cairn is at the centre of a group of such funerary monuments. 99-cs-1797

metal smelting activity in the Medieval period, when monasteries are known to have been drawing incomes from extensive upland mining at Cwmystwyth and possibly Esgair-Mwyn in upland north Ceredigion, and elsewhere. Sampling of the upper levels of peat bogs can also be a useful source of information in determining management and conservation strategies (Caseldine 2002).

Environmental archaeology has a key role to play in providing additional information on what happened in the uplands in any one period and in providing a context for the more detailed site information that is currently being gained from the Uplands Initiative. It is an approach that can help to create a wider picture of contemporary societies and their legacies than excavation and survey alone can do.

Another technique of potentially wide application is the DNA testing of residual populations. Preliminary results show that most of the genetic types of Europe are pre-Neolithic and have lived in the same upland and lowland localities for at least 6000 years. Populations derived from the original Palaeolithic (Old Stone Age) hunter-gatherer inhabitants were already well-established before relatively few Neolithic farmers moved across the continent introducing the new methods of agriculture and revolutionising the use of the uplands and the lowlands alike. Genetics has answered a question which could not have been answered by traditional archaeological and historical methods. However, further work along these lines must be done before the ever-increasing mobility of populations makes such testing difficult, if not impossible (Sykes 1999a and b; Lewin 1997).

Some of the initial work on DNA has already established links between the upland populations of the Basque region and of Wales. The Basques speak a Stone Age, non-Indo-European language that seems to be earlier than Welsh. However, the majority of the people of Wales, especially those of the uplands, share male ('Y') chromosomes that are indistinguishable from the Basque population as well as those of Ireland, the Scottish mainland and most of the south and west of England (including Cornwall). This suggests that the arrival of the Celtic language family did not involve the replacement of the male population by immigration from the

east. The key to understanding this language change is in the Celtic female, or 'mt', DNA, which is different from that of the Basques but similar to that of the rest of Europe. The obvious deduction from this is that women were much more mobile than men. A related factor may have been warfare, endemic to much of prehistoric society, as evidenced by the proliferation of upland hillforts. Women would often have been taken captive and intermarriage would also have been necessary to cement alliances between neighbouring tribes and peoples. In this way mother tongues were changed (www.bbc.co.uk/history). The remoteness of the Welsh Uplands has, in its turn, ensured the survival of the Welsh language into the modern period as Celtic languages elsewhere in Europe fell out of use.

It is only in the uplands that we are left with anything approaching the intact landscapes that accompanied the momentous changes that have determined the character of modern Wales, and indeed the whole of Europe. It is essential in future work that the various skills of the archaeologist, historian, environmental scientist and geneticist be used in close combination if we are to arrive at a fuller picture of the factors and processes that have produced the landscape and culture of the Welsh uplands in their present form.

At the present rate of progress it should be possible to complete on two levels the archaeological survey of all the unenclosed uplands of Wales within ten years. All significant sites will have been located by ground survey and entered on the National Database by 2012. Detailed work on the ground is an essential tool of archaeological reconnaissance and is especially valuable for locating small isolated features that are not recognisable from the air, such as Bronze Age burial cairns. However, it is aerial photography that allows an overview of all sites in the landscape to be made and which allows linear features such as early field boundaries, artificial watercourses and transport ways to be made sense of and plotted on digitised maps. Equally, the groundwork funded from the Initiative validates office-based mapping where roads, watercourses and significant linear features are largely indistinguishable.

The future also promises the possibility of the full integration of both historical and aerial mapping with ground-based fieldwork. At the present we have partial information

Black Mountains: the unspoilt nature of the uplands is evident in this winter scene of the Black Mountains south of Hay-on-Wye (Y Gelli), showing Lord Hereford's Knob from Waun Croes Hywel. The wandering edge between the intensively 'improved' and enclosed lowlands and the relict uplands is clear. 2001-cs-0807

based on the segment of the uplands already surveyed and the beginning of an understanding of what it all means. The continuance of systematic and large-scale work promises a much deeper overall understanding of the size and relative distribution of the archaeological resource and its significance.

There can be a full use of new methodologies including scientific archaeology. Satellites can be used to fix the location of remote sites using global positioning system (GPS) equipment. Cores from peat will not only be used to yield results for pollen analysis but will be subjected to a range of geochemical analyses which will reveal where people were smelting (and hence mining) minerals in the uplands throughout the prehistoric and historic eras. The value of such environmental archaeology will be greatly increased by relating it to the soil layers (stratigraphy) revealed by excavations carried out nearby. There is great potential for increased understanding of distinct types of upland archaeological sites by substantial excavations of settlement sites. DNA testing of indigenous upland populations, before the rapid population movements of the modern world dilute them further, has the value of revealing just how much the uplands have sheltered earlier population groups from the more mixed populations of the lowlands of Europe.

A very wide range of society – government agencies, local authorities, utility groups and, not least, local communities – has a role and responsibility in understanding, interpreting and managing change in the landscape. The Uplands Initiative will continue to provide archaeological information that will allow an interaction with general society to create a wider and deeper understanding and vision and achieve a balance between conservation and economic development. The Initiative will continue to facilitate a sustainable future by allowing more information to drive a shift from reactive and protectionist measures based on partial knowledge of the archaeological resource towards more creative and proactive management strategies based on a fuller knowledge and understanding of what sites and types of monument exist in the uplands.

The Uplands Archaeology Initiative will help to make the uplands a more generally appreciated resource. The use of information and knowledge will be facilitated by making data about and pictures of sites widely available on the internet within six months of the completion of archaeological fieldwork. There will be a future use of information directly obtainable in the field: detailed site information will be available via portable computers and at centres developed in partnership. Work on the first heritage education centre interpreting an upland landscape has begun in partnership with Torfaen County Borough Council at St Peter's School in Blaenafon, and there are opportunities for more to be developed in other areas. The ready availability of significant amounts of information will change and inform opinions. The new technology is the best hope for safeguarding archaeological sites for the future. If people can be given understanding of what individual monuments represent and why they are considered important they are more likely to respect and preserve them.

A review of the Uplands Initiative is available on the internet at www.rcahmw.org.uk and this is updated continually with a map of project areas, full bibliography and database.

The development and standardisation of types of site-name and glossaries for uplands archaeology now allow for the first time a retrieval and perception of general trends and the overall distribution of specific types of upland site throughout Wales. As the Initiative progresses towards completion it will be possible to generate meaningful distribution maps of densities of particular site-types throughout Wales and to consider their meaning for its history.

How can upland society generally benefit from these developments? Walking in Wales is already estimated to generate £40,000,000 per annum into the rural economy. The rich archaeological heritage that has been revealed by the Uplands Initiative can be a main selling-point in attracting interest and visitors to the uplands of Wales. The development of way-marked trails provided with introductory leaflets and information signboards is one way to optimise this potential, and such developments are currently taking place on the Ceredigion uplands at Cwmystwyth and on the uplands landscape of the World Heritage Site at Blaenafon. Both developments have been steered by partnerships of organisations reflecting the full range of bodies representing both the natural and human heritage of the Welsh uplands. This work has been described elsewhere in this volume and provides a blueprint of what can be achieved throughout Wales in a move that would improve the sustainable economy of communities in the uplands.

Countryside management is not about fossilising change: landscapes are dynamic and the changing relationship between people through time will continue to create new landscapes. Readily available information and knowledge of the archaeology of the uplands will allow a sustainable, integrated and holistic approach to the management of the rich historic landscapes that surround every upland community, and help them tap a hitherto largely unrealised and undeveloped resource that can support them into the future.

AN ILLUSTRATED GUIDE TO COMMON FIELD MONUMENTS

Robert Silvester (Clwyd-Powys Archaeological Trust)

Throughout this monograph the authors have alluded to various types of upland monument, and *An Upland Glossary for Wales* was prepared recently to assist in the classification of the full range of monuments (Sambrook 2000). The following section offers a rudimentary guide to field monuments in the Welsh uplands, some types encountered in virtually every upland survey, others rather less commonly. The guide cannot be exhaustive, for both the nature of the archaeology and the space available prohibit any attempt at comprehensiveness, and there is in any case an extensive literature on some monument types, particularly those of prehistoric date. By comparison information on the upland field monuments of more recent origin is rather sparse. In this chapter monument types have been grouped together according to their nature or their function, and the brief descriptions are backed up by illustrations and also by references to readily accessible publications where there are more discursive texts on Welsh sites. Many of these monuments are also likely to be found in upland regions elsewhere, and so in some instances particularly useful examples have been cited from further afield.

Stone settings

Stone circles, stone rows and other less regular settings of upright stones are not uncommon in the Welsh uplands. Both the stones themselves and the monuments created from them are of varying size. Conventionally most are attributed to the Bronze Age, but stone circles were built in modern times too – witness the *gorsedd* circles in many Welsh towns. Occasionally recently constructed and anonymous settings of stones have been found in the uplands, as for example a circle incorporating a decorated stone on a common in northern Radnorshire.

Many standing stones are presumed to be prehistoric, yet intrinsically they are almost impossible to date. Large stones, to several metres in height, are likely to be Bronze Age, but

Gors Fawr stone circle, Mynachlog Ddu, Pembrokeshire. A circle of 16 stones standing up to a metre high, erected on a tract of wind-swept moorland within sight of the Preseli Mountains. 2002-cs-4015

smaller examples potentially have a much wider range of functions and dates. Stone gateposts in abandoned boundaries should be fairly obvious, as are in many cases, though not all, stone boundary markers, whether for parishes or estates (see below). Naturally-occurring upright blocks of stone can confuse, as can rubbing posts set up by farmers for their stock.

For stone circles see Bowen and Gresham 1967, 34. For the embanked stone circle known as the Druid's Circle at Penmaenmawr see RCAHMW 1956, 89; Darvill 1986, 10; and Crew and Musson 1996, 11. Other good examples come from Brecknocks: RCAHMW 1997, 147; and Leighton 1997, 62. For stone rows see illustrations in Burnham 1995, 36 and 46; and Leighton 1997, 79. For a useful discussion on standing stones see RCAHMW 1997, 162.

Carreg Waun Llech standing stone, Brecknocks. 261000/0031/22

Cairns

It can be difficult to ascertain with certainty whether or not simple cairns of heaped stone represent prehistoric burial sites. Greater certainty attaches to the more complex cairns incorporating kerbs of upright stones or cists where stone slabs are set on edge to create grave pits, and to those special forms of burial monument which collectively are known as ring cairns. Most of these monuments are of Bronze Age origin, and those of earlier, Neolithic date such as chambered long and round cairns are very much rarer. Burial in cairns did occur at other times, as in the early medieval era, though normally this involved the re-use of Bronze Age monuments.

Clearance cairns, the residue of clearing stones usually, though not exclusively, from arable land can be of various, often irregular shapes, including linear arrangements, and may have originated at any time from the prehistoric era through to the immediate past. Where clustered they tend to be termed cairnfields, particularly if they are considered to be of prehistoric origin; the cairns may on occasion be the only indicator of arable activity.

Other cairn types, normally of post-medieval or modern origin, include marker cairns on boundaries and walkers' cairns in prominent locations.

Useful plans and descriptions of upland cairns appear in the Brenig Valley excavation report (Lynch 1993, 41ff; 135ff; see also Burnham 1995, 25); in studies of Brecknocks (RCAHMW 1997, 69; Leighton 1997, 65; 70); in the classic description of Merioneth (Bowen and Gresham 1967, 72); in *Archaeologia Cambrensis* (e.g. Marshall and Murphy 1991); and in photographs elsewhere (Crew and Musson 1996, 11). For examples from further afield see Johnson and Rose 1994, 34 for Bodmin Moor; and for a typology see also Lynch 1979. For chambered cairns from Brecknocks see Burnham 1995, 13 and RCAHMW 1997, 31; and from Merioneth see Bowen and Gresham 1967, 4. For cairnfields see plans and descriptions in the Brenig Valley excavation report (Lynch 1993, 161) and also in reports of excavations in Glamorgan (Lawler *et al.* 1997). For other descriptions see Kelly 1982, 132; Manley 1990, 517; Leighton 1997, 91; and for Scottish parallels see also Wickham-Jones 2001, 48.

Hut circles

Prehistoric house sites are usually described as hut circles, though as an alternative 'round house' is used, particularly for excavated examples. Appearing as circular banks of stone,

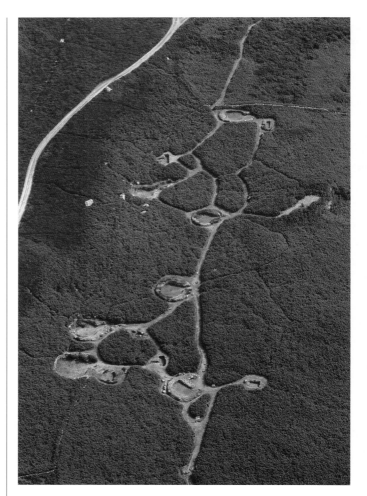

Part of the Ty Mawr hut group near Holyhead on Anglesey, first excavated between 1862-8 by the Hon. W.O. Stanley. The large, round-stone house walls once supported conical timber roofs, while the smaller rectangular buildings are thought to have been workshops, producing evidence for metal working. The buildings were principally occupied during the Iron Age with reuse up to the sixth century AD. 95-cs-1798

interrupted by entrance gaps, they often display facing or revetment slabs, although the material is often disguised by grass or other vegetation. They tend to be more commonly encountered where surface stone is plentiful, as in north-west Wales and the Brecon Beacons, and are less obvious in uplands where other building materials may have been adopted. Numbers can vary from single huts to large groups, be unenclosed or set within an enclosure, and be associated with fields, paddocks, tracks and others elements that make up a farming landscape. In date they range from the Bronze Age

Hut circles at Crawcwellt near Trawsfynydd in Snowdonia. Excavations at this wind-swept site have revealed evidence for early iron production, dating from about 300 BC to the Roman conquest. The excavated huts have been reconstructed for public viewing. 2001-cs-2051

to the Roman or perhaps the early medieval centuries. Some may have been used seasonally.

Excavated examples include Cyfannyd, Arthog, within a circular enclosure (Darvill 1986, 31). For descriptions see Leighton 1997, 80 and Kelly 1982, 139. For illustrations in Snowdonia see Crew and Musson 1996, 14; Bowen and Gresham 1967, 178; and Kelly 1982, 148. The RCAHMW volumes for Caernarvonshire (1956-64) depict numerous examples of both enclosed and unenclosed hut circles (but see particularly RCAHMW 1964, lxxxvii), and there is a recent re-assessment in Smith 1999. For a discussion on seasonal use see Kelly 1982, 141.

Hillforts and enclosures

Defensive or protective enclosures known as hillforts are found sporadically throughout the Welsh uplands and are amongst the best known monuments in Wales. With one or more earth or stone lines of defence, often of substantial proportions and enclosing up to several hectares, examples in the uplands are likely to show habitation sites in the form

either of hut circles or scoops (see below under platforms). Hillforts are usually considered to be of first millennium BC date, with some, on excavation, revealing re-use late in the Roman period and into the succeeding early medieval era.

The term enclosure is widely used for anything from an embanked parcel of land of no more than a few square metres to areas which are equivalent in size to fields, and with a date range extending from the prehistoric period through to recent centuries. They may be bounded by stone walls, earthen banks or a combination of the two, and be accompanied by an external ditch. Some functioned as home- or farmstead enclosures and are best seen as diminutive cousins of the hillforts, while smaller enclosures may also have housed either humans or stock (cf. sheepfolds). Other enclosures may have had specialist functions, such as monastic granges and enclosed sheepcotes, or some industrial purpose. A wide range of functions is possible and not all enclosures can be readily interpreted or dated simply from field observations.

There is a sizeable literature on hillforts. Amongst others see Bowen and Gresham 1967, 129; RCAHMW 1986; Musson 1994, 52; Crew and Musson 1996, 9; and Burnham 1995, 58. For enclosures see Bowen and Gresham 1967, 206 and RCAHMW 1982, 365 and pl. 7. For monastic granges see Williams 2001, 192, and for a specific upland example Silvester 1997. For sheepcotes see Dyer 1995, and more specifically see Gresham *et al.* 1959 and Musson 1994, 122 for Hen Ddinbych.

Burnt mounds and others

Normally known as burnt mounds, but in the past as boiling mounds, these often distinctive heaps of burnt and fractured stone, circular or crescentic in shape, can indicate hearths or cooking places, though in the past other interpretations have been advanced, including the possibility that some functioned as prehistoric saunas. Where excavated they have usually been found to be Bronze Age in date, although early medieval examples are known from near Aberaeron in Ceredigion.

Mounds are commonplace in the uplands. Many may have a natural origin – a grass-covered rock outcrop for instance – while others may have resulted from activities as diverse as burial and industry.

For useful discussions see RCAHMW 1997, 184; Leighton 1997, 93; and Bowen and Gresham 1967, 286. For the early medieval burnt mound see Williams 1985; for medieval slag mounds associated with iron working see Smith 1995. For Scottish burnt mounds see Wickham-Jones 2001, 66.

Platforms

Deliberately constructed platforms can have several different origins, and in the absence of excavation it can be only their shape and associations that provide some guidance to their date. By their general nature they are likely to have a scarped slope at the rear where the platform has been levelled into the slope; and at the front (i.e. the downhill side) the ground may be artificially built up to increase the size of the flat platform. Platforms may display the remains of buildings on them.

A circular or sub-circular platform is more likely to be prehistoric, probably Bronze Age or Iron Age, or perhaps even later, and to have formed the base for a hut circle. Long known within hillforts, these are increasingly being recognised in unenclosed locations in the hills throughout Wales. Allied to these circular platforms are scoops of sub-circular and semicircular form.

A rectangular platform set at right angles to the contour and with material built up at the front almost certainly formed the stance for a house or farm building of medieval or early post-medieval date. Rectangular platforms which lie along the contour are more likely to be post-medieval than earlier. Such platforms are found throughout the Welsh uplands but appear to be more common in a band running from the Glamorgan uplands through Powys and into Denbighshire and Meirionnydd.

Shallow quarries of relatively recent date can display similar surface characteristics to platforms, and in extreme cases it may not be possible to distinguish between the two. Spring-heads and natural erosion may also create features which superficially are very similar to artificial platforms.

For examples of platforms within hillforts see Pen-y-gaer (RCAHMW 1960, 104); and for elsewhere see Manley 1986; Leighton 1997, 86; and Wickham-Jones 2001, 28 (Scotland). For scoops see examples from Brecknocks (RCAHMW 1997, 201) and Gwynedd (GAT 1993/4). For rectangular platforms see Gresham 1954; RCAHMW 1982, 17 with plans and pls.; and Leighton 1997, 102. For examples in Snowdonia see Crew and Musson 1996, 40. For excavated examples see Courtney 1991.

Roman military activity

Permanently garrisoned Roman forts tended to occupy the more hospitable valleys rather than the uplands above them. Temporary marching camps, some covering several hectares, can appear in remote moorlands, as can fortlets and practice camps. Roman roads, which were initially constructed during the military period, often passed through the uplands, and some of the best-preserved examples are to be found in such environments.

For examples in the uplands around the Elan Valley and in the western Brecon Beacons see Musson 1994, 136ff and RCAHMW 1986, 150; and for Snowdonia, Crew and Musson 1996, 28. See also Burnham 1995, 80 & 84 and Davies 1986. For roads see Bowen and Gresham 1967, 246 and RCAHMW 1986, 157.

Long-huts, cottages and other buildings

Rectangular stone-built huts are a common discovery in many upland surveys, their walls surviving to a low height or perhaps only as grass-covered foundations. Their function, their seasonal utilisation and even their date can be a matter of some debate. Many may have been used only in the summer

The remains of a long-house, discovered along a tributary of the Car valley by the Assistant Range Officer of Sennybridge, and subsequently recorded as part of the Cadw-funded Deserted Rural Settlements Project. © Clwyd Powys Archaeological Trust ref. CPAT C5/00/47/29

months as *hafodydd or lluestydd*, while others may have been occupied permanently and may even have functioned as true longhouses with man and beast housed under the same roof. In some cases what started as a temporary residence may have become a permanent steading. While the possibility exists that some may go back into the early medieval era, the majority are

Carnfachbugeilyn. On one of the high ridges of the Pumlumon range, straddling the county boundary between Ceredigion and Montgomeryshire, Bronze Age people built the lonely burial cairn of Carnfachbugeilyn not far above the source of the River Severn. Despite the comparatively remote situation of many such burial mounds, they nevertheless continue to act as focal points in the landscape for walkers, hill farmers and even soldiers on manoeuvres. This cairn has been quite heavily mutilated with the construction of a dry stone shelter on one part. Arcs of stone visible immediately in front of the shelter may represent the original structural walls or kerbs of the denuded Bronze Age cairn. 98-cs-0882

likely to be medieval or even more likely post-medieval in date. Here the concept of the *ty unnos* (the dwelling built in one night) is central to the process of encroachment and squatting on the open uplands in the post-medieval centuries. The foundations and ruins of many such small buildings and their successors are to be found throughout the uplands.

Other rectangular structures of not dissimilar form include field cowhouses, the modern equivalent of which can still be found in some Welsh uplands.

See RCAHMW 1982, 43; Cadw 2002; and Newman *et al.* 2001, 129. For *hafodydd* and the like see the Cadw volume on deserted rural settlement (forthcoming) and also Leighton 1997, 100. The main excavation on a *hafod* site is that at the Brenig (Allen 1979; Musson 1994, 123); although for an alternative view see RCAHMW 1997, 202. For cowhouses and the like see plans and descriptions in the Brenig Valley excavation report (Lynch 1993, 181) and also Wiliam 1986, 89.

Shelters

Common in the uplands are roughly built drystone structures, usually of irregular design, often integrating natural features such as rock outcrops, and with small internal areas, which go under the general name of shelters. They are likely to have been constructed by shepherds, peat cutters and indeed anyone

who exploited the resources of the uplands. Most are likely to have originated in the post-medieval centuries, but no doubt reflect a practice which had much earlier origins. Large and prominent cairns frequently have their rubble shifted to create modern shelters, and such re-use can also be detected at other field monuments.

See Leighton 1997, 47, and also Johnson and Rose 1994, 80 for discussion of examples from Bodmin Moor, England.

Sunken stores and pens

Stone-built stores encased in earthen mounds may be confused with prehistoric chambered cairns by the unwary. Usually found close to abandoned cottages and farms they are often carefully constructed and were used for storage of potatoes and perhaps other root crops. Sometimes they are known as potato 'hogs'. The earthwork equivalent of the store, the clamp, often appears in small groups of two or more rectangular depressions with earth piled around the rim or to one side. More simple stone-built stores may also be found in association with seasonally occupied long-huts (*qv*) in certain areas of the Welsh uplands where they were used for preserving dairy products.

Circular structures may have acted as animal pens, some better preserved examples remaining on a few upland farms.

See Leighton 1997, 102 and Wiliam 1986, 28.

Folds and other stock features

Sheepfolds appear in various guises, few of which are still in use; most are drystone-built, though 'post-and-wire' types have become more prevalent in recent times. In Snowdonia there are complex folds consisting of many 'cells', and such multi-cellular structures are occasionally found elsewhere, indicative of the co-operative efforts of sheep farmers and the mixing of flocks on the open hills. Circular sheepfolds, akin to the stells of Scotland, appear, but only intermittently. Much more common are the rectilinear drystone folds, often crudely built, with one or two compartments. Their earthen counterparts are less readily recognisable, but do exist in some places, particularly where surface stone is less easily available; they normally consist of a low bank which may originally have been surmounted by wooden palings or something similar. Folds are often found in upland valleys, close to well-used tracks or in sheltered locations such as at the foot of a slope.

Sheep dips and/or washing pens can be associated with folds but may appear as ponded areas within streams, and there may be associated earthworks such as holding pens, funnels for channeling the stock and dams for holding back the water.

Shelter walls, again drystone-built, were often constructed in exposed areas to provide protection for stock, although they are much more prevalent in some regions than others. The Denbigh Moors for instance are littered with examples, and there they appear in a variety of forms from the simple I shape to those forming a T, L and even more complex outlines.

For multi-cellular folds see RCAHMW 1956, lxxvii and Leighton 1997, 46; for an aerial view see Crew and Musson 1996, 42. For less complex examples see the Brenig Valley excavation report (Lynch 1993, 181). For washing pens see Winchester 2000, 59.

Warrens and pillow mounds

Indicative of rabbit farming, warrens are identified by the presence of 'pillow mounds'. These appear in several guises. Long and relatively narrow earthen banks are the commonest and may cover artificially constructed burrows; pillow-shaped mounds are probably commoner in parts of southern England but do show occasionally in Wales, and cruciform mounds also appear. Large circular mounds may also have served as warrens, but the presence of small earthen mounds in a warren reflects a different aspect of rabbit farming, for these perhaps formed the bases for posts on which traps were placed to catch the raptors that preyed on the rabbits. Some mounds are found

Multi-cellular sheepfold in the Anafon valley in Gwynedd.
94-cs-1112

in isolation, and groups of several mounds are common. Larger groups of thirty mounds and upwards also occur occasionally and may be accompanied by the foundations of warreners' houses and perhaps vermin traps. Several large warrens in the Brecon Beacons with between forty and eighty-five mounds lie within large enclosures and have traps to catch the rabbits, but these are unusual and imply rabbit farming at

Warrens and pillow mounds. Circular and cigar-shaped pillow mounds on Coed Swydd common in central Powys, partly overlain by ridge-and-furrow cultivation. 99-cs-0126

a commercial level, as much perhaps for the skins as for the meat. Where dated these warrens are usually of eighteenth- or even nineteenth-century date, though a medieval date has been postulated for a warren near Lampeter (Ceredigion).

For pillow mounds see RCAHMW 1982, 313 (with plans and a now out-of-date distribution map of pillow mounds in Wales); Austin 1988; and Silvester 1995. For illustrations see Musson 1994, 150ff and Leighton 1997, 43. For vermin traps see Austin 1988, 155. For the larger sites see RCAHMW 1982 and Leighton 1997, 43; and for traps see Harris and Spratt 1991. For the medieval sites see Austin 1988.

Peat-cutting

Peat extraction has a long history going back into the medieval era, and the cuttings, otherwise known as turbaries and generally presumed to be of more recent date, can leave extensive traces often more apparent from the air than on the ground. The cuttings, usually linear, can aggregate into blocks of parallel hollows, but there are exceptions of irregular outline such as the mawn pits on the Radnorshire commons (Welsh *mawn* = peat). Abandoned peat stacks showing as mounds are not uncommon. Peat-drying platforms may remain as earthworks, sometimes ditched, but in north-west Wales there are sub-oval stony platforms known as peat stools, no more than one course of stone high. In a few places in Caernarvonshire stone-built peat houses functioned as storage places. The presence of well-defined tracks and holloways will often indicate the nearby location of a heavily exploited turbary.

For descriptions see Owen 1969; 1975; 1990. For peat-drying platforms see RCAHMW 1956, lxxviii and Crew and Musson 1996, 43. For peat houses see RCAHMW 1956, lxxviii; and for comparable sites in northern England see Winchester 2000, 130.

Leisure

Common in many uplands are butts or hides, evidence of grouse shooting on the open moors from the later nineteenth century onwards. Normally of earth and peat but sometimes with stone, these are usually small, sub-circular embanked enclosures. They can appear as solitary examples, but also in lines of eight, nine or more.

Other leisure activities may occasionally leave their imprint on the uplands. Golf courses are not unknown, and even the sites of former race courses are found.

Little has been written about Welsh examples. For a more general comment see Newman *et al.* 2001, 119. For an aerial view of an abandoned golf course just over the border in Shropshire see Musson 1993, 12.

Tracks

Tracks and paths appear in various forms: holloways or hollow trails, where constant use has resulted in the gradual lowering of the track to a linear hollow; sled tracks; terraceways, where the track traverses a slope creating a linear terrace; packhorse trails; roads of Roman date (*qv*); and braided trackways, where the erosion of tracks through continuous use on slopes necessitated the steady creation of further new paths up or down the slope. The date range can be from, putatively, the prehistoric centuries through to the early modern era of turnpike roads and twentieth-century agricultural tracks.

For holloways see RCAHMW 1982, 347 and Moore-Colyer 2001, 74. For a description of packhorse trails see RCAHMW 1960, lxv. For braided tracks see Musson 1994, 151 and Leighton 1997, 50. For prehistoric trackways see Bowen and Gresham 1967, 36. For a medieval track with a monastic use see Moore-Colyer 2001, 73. For a disused upland turnpike see Leighton 1997, 49

Boundaries, dykes and other linear earthworks

Banks with or without accompanying ditches are a common upland phenomenon. These can be of earth, stone or a mixture of these materials. Terminology can vary from area to area, so, for instance, in Gwynedd both ditches and banks are often referred to by the Welsh term *clawdd* (pl. *cloddiau*). Many may be no more than the boundaries of enclosures captured from the waste in the post-medieval centuries, but some are perhaps earlier. Those separating the open hill grazings from enclosed land and known variously as mountain walls, head dykes, or even (as in south-west England) corn dykes, can be rather more massive than the usual boundary.

Dating is not always straightforward. Some may be prehistoric, others medieval or post-medieval, and some linear boundaries such as the stony bank running for over one kilometre across Llangynidr Common in southern Powys remain enigmatic.

More specific origins include manorial and township boundaries, and monastic grange boundaries. Parish and estate boundaries in the uplands were sometimes distinguished only by natural features or even by no more than notional lines on a map. At other times stones, sometimes inscribed with the initials of the landowner, the name of the parish and occasionally a date, were set up at regular intervals across the open uplands. Many are nineteenth-century, but others can be assigned to the eighteenth century.

In south-east Wales and the Welsh borderland short or cross-dykes are occasionally encountered, banks often with an accompanying ditch running across a spur or a ridge, sometimes from the head of one valley to the head of another. The size may vary from massive earthworks to much smaller examples, which in their physical characteristics are little different from field boundaries. What singles them out is their linearity. Few can be accurately dated, but there are reasons to believe that some are of Bronze Age or Iron Age origin, some early medieval, whilst others still could be of later medieval date.

For useful discussions see Leighton 1997, 29, and from elsewhere Winchester 2000, 53. For prehistoric tracks see Ward 1989. For short dykes see Burnham 1995, 117 and Musson 1993, 25.

Fields and cultivation

Fields can range in date from the Bronze Age through to the early modern era, and come in different forms. Prehistoric fields can be regular in shape but can also be defined by

On Kerry Hill in upland Montgomeryshire, a well-preserved cross dyke passes close to Two Tumps Bronze Age barrows (centre left). 2001-cs-0417

'wandering walls', though these may also have delimited pastoral enclosures (*qv*). The phenomenon of lynchet formation, whereby material is ploughed away or builds up to create a scarp, is common to all periods.

The corrugated surface left by heaping up soil, either by hand or by plough action, to create areas for cultivation occurs frequently in the uplands. Ridges covering areas of only a few square metres may be 'lazy beds' resulting from spade cultivation in the vicinity of a hut or cottage. Large areas of regular ridging may result from the continued ploughing of new intakes and enclosures, subsequently abandoned. Some cultivation ridges may be medieval in date, and enclosures too may be ridged. On the open commons much greater areas of ridging result from what in central Wales was termed 'betting', the taking of a crop from newly ploughed ground for perhaps

Alexandra Slate Quarry (1860s - 1980s): a typical Cwm Nantlle quarry-pit on unenclosed upland, once employing over two hundred people to produce six thousand tons of slate a year. A powered incline, visible at the lower left of the flooded quarry, hoisted slate to the steam-powered dressing-sheds. A locomotive railway led over the mountain to the main Welsh Highland Railway at Betws Garmon. Huge spoil tips radiate from the pit at the top right, centre left and bottom. 99-cs-2025

two or three years before allowing the ground to revert to the moor.

Occasionally no ridging occurs, but the ground is divided into beds by narrow slits or channels, presumably to facilitate drainage.

Much of the cultivation ridging is likely to be post-medieval in origin. In some places it can be medieval, but usually this can be determined only by its association with other, better dated, features. The possibility of prehistoric ridging should also be born in mind, comparable perhaps with the late prehistoric cord rig of northern England, but as yet this does not seem to be well evidenced in Wales.

For prehistoric fields see Musson 1994, 82; Crew and Musson 1996, 20; and RCAHMW 1960, 35 and 48. For lazy beds see a hut group at Caerhun (Caernarfon) in RCAHMW 1956, 30. For medieval ridging in Snowdonia see Crew and Musson 1996, 41; on the Berwyn see this volume (page 81, Silvester 2000); and on the north Wales coast see Aris 1996, 58. For post-medieval cultivation of the uplands see Musson 1994, 152. For ridged enclosures see Leighton 1997, 34.

Mining and quarrying

Lead, copper, silver and gold were all mined in Wales, in some places on a huge scale. It is generally believed that copper was extracted from the Bronze Age onwards, but the greatest impact on the landscape was in recent centuries. Metal mine remains may encompass a whole range of site types and workings, some showing as structures, others as earthworks, and there is an extensive literature relevant to them. The visible remains may include buildings with various functions: trials, which were used for prospecting for minerals; working floors; spoil tips; reservoirs (*qv*); hushings, where water was diverted over the ground surface to wash away the overburden exposing mineral veins beneath; and horizontal tunnels known as adits and vertical shafts

Quarrying can range from massive disturbance of the landscape down to small-scale surface works, and again encompass many centuries from the Neolithic through to the twentieth century. While many quarries cover irregular tracts some that followed particular rock seams appear as linear scars. Limestone extraction created its own set of distinctive remains, whether the quarries and spoil heaps, kiln groups or the isolated field kilns.

For good aerial views of mining see Musson 1994, 72 and Hudson 1984, 19. For quarries see Musson 1994, 97 and 137; Crew and Musson 1996, 49 and 53; and Leighton 1997, 42. For kilns see Leighton 1997, 37.

Leats and reservoirs

Reservoirs have been created in the uplands to provide water supplies, often by the construction of a dam across a watercourse and usually for industrial purposes. Water might also be diverted off the headwaters of a stream and down an artificially constructed channel known as a leat, which followed the contours and provided a more convenient supply to an industrial site or sometimes a farm.

UPLANDS BIBLIOGRAPHY

Aldhouse-Green, S. 2000. Palaeolithic and Mesolithic Wales, in Lynch, Aldhouse-Green and Davies 2000, 1-41.

Aldhouse-Green, S. 2001. *Paviland Cave and the 'Red' Lady: A definitive report*, Bristol: SCARAB, University of Wales, Newport and the Friends of the National Museum of Wales Cardiff.

Allen, D. 1979. Excavations at Hafod y Nant Criafolen, Brenig Valley, Clwyd, 1973-4, *Post-Medieval Archaeology* 13, 1-59.

Aris, M. 1996. *Historic landscapes of the Great Orme*, Llanrwst: Gwasg Carreg Gwalch.

Arnold, C. J. and Davies, J. L. 2000. *Roman and Early Medieval Wales*, Stroud: Sutton Publishing.

Austin, D. 1988. Excavations and survey at Bryn Cysegrfan, Llanfair Clydogau, Dyfed, 1979, *Medieval Archaeology* 23, 130-165.

Avery, M. 1993. *Hillfort Defences of Southern Britain*, Oxford: British Archaeological Reports, British Series 231.

Bailey, M. 1991. *Per impetum maris*: natural disaster and economic decline in eastern England, 1275-1350, in Campbell, B. M. S. (ed) *Before the Black Death: studies in the 'crisis' of the early fourteenth century*, Manchester: Manchester University Press, 184-208.

Barker, C. T. 1992. *The Chambered Tombs of South-west Wales*, Oxford: Oxbow Monograph 14.

Barton, R. N. E., Berridge, P. J., Walker, M. J. C. and Bevins, R. E. 1995. Persistent Places in the Mesolithic Landscape: an example from the Black Mountain uplands of South Wales, *Proceedings of the Prehistoric Society* 61, 81-116.

Bassett, T. M. and Davies, B. L. (eds) 1972. *Atlas of Caernarvonshire*, Caernarfon: Gwynedd Rural Council.

Bell, M. 1989. Environmental archaeology as an index of continuity and change in the medieval landscape, in Aston, M., Austin, D. and Dyer, C. (eds) *The rural settlements of medieval England*, Oxford: Basil Blackwell, 269-86.

Bell, M. G. and Dark, P. 1998. Continuity and change: environmental archaeology in historic periods, in Bayley, J. (ed) *Science in Archaeology*, London: English Heritage, 179-94.

Berry, A. Q. 1990. The parks and forests of the lordship of Dyffryn Clwyd, *Denbighshire Historical Society Transactions* 43, 7-25.

Bewley, R. H. 1997. Aerial Photography for Archaeology, in Hunter, J. and Ralston, I. (eds) *Archaeological Resource Management in the UK - An Introduction*, Stroud: Sutton Publishing, 197-204.

Bick, D. E. 1976. *The Old Metal Mines of Mid-Wales: Part 3 - Cardiganshire - North of Goginan*, Newent, Glos.: The Pound House.

Bick, D. E. 1978. *The Old Metal Mines of Mid-Wales: Part 5 - Aberdovey, Dinas Mawddwy and Llangynog*, Newent, Glos.: The Pound House.

Bick, D. E. 1990. Observations on Ancient Mining in Wales, in Crew, P. and Crew, S. (eds) *Early Mining in the British Isles*, Maentwrog: Snowdonia National Park Study Centre, Occasional Paper 1, 75-7.

Bick, D. E. 1993. *The Old Metal Mines of Mid-Wales*: *Combined Edition Parts 1-6*, Newent, Glos.: The Pound House.

Bick, D. E. 1994. Early Mining Leats and Ponds in Wales, in Ford, T. and Willies, L. (eds) Mining Before Powder, *Bulletin Peak District Mines Historical Society* 12: 3, 37-40.

Blaenafon Aerial Mapping, National Monuments Record of Wales, Aberystwyth.

Blaenavon 1999. *Management Plan. Blaenavon Industrial Landscape*, Torfaen: The Blaenavon Partnership.

Bowen, E. G. and Gresham, C. A. 1967. *History of Merioneth, Volume I: from the earliest times to the Age of the Native Princes*, Dolgellau: Merioneth Historical and Record Society.

Boyd, J. I. C. 1981. *Narrow Gauge Railways in North Caernarvonshire Vol. I - West*, Trowbridge: Oakwood.

Briggs, C. S. 1985. Problems of the Early Agricultural Landscape in Upland Wales as illustrated by an example from the Brecon Beacons, in Burgess, C. B. and Spratt, D. A. (eds) *Upland Settlement in Britain,* Oxford: British Archaeological Reports, British Series 143, 285-315.

Briggs, C. S. 1991a. Some Processes and Problems in Later Prehistoric Wales and Beyond, in Chevillot, C. and Coffyn, A. (eds) *Le Bronze Atlantique, Actes du Ier colloque du Parc Archeologique de Beynac*, Beynac-Cazenac, Dordogne, 59-76.

Briggs, C. S. 1991b. Garden Archaeology in Wales: a review, in Brown, A. E. (ed) *Garden Archaeology,* London: Council for British Archaeology, CBA Research Report 78.

Briggs, C. S. 1991c. Early Mines in Wales: the date of Copa Hill, *Archaeology in Wales* 31, 5-7.

Briggs, C. S. 1994. Sennybridge Training Area - A Fossil Agricultural Landscape, *Sanctuary* 23, 13-4.

Briggs, C. S. 1994a. Reply to Budd *et al.* on Ancient Mines, *Archaeology in Wales* 34, 13-5.

Briggs, C. S. 1994b. The Bronze Age, in Davies, J. L. and Kirby, D. J. (eds) *The County History of Cardiganshire, Vol. 1*, Cardiff: University of Wales Press, 124-218.

Briggs, C. S. (ed) 2003. *Towards a Research Agenda for Welsh Archaeology*, Oxford: British Archaeological Reports, British Series 343.

Briggs, C. S. 2003. A Strategy for Raw Materials in Welsh Archaeology, in Briggs (ed) 2003, 201-11.

Britnell, W. J. and Savory, H. N. 1984. *Gwernvale and Penywrlod: Two Neolithic Long Cairns in the Black Mountains of Brecknock*, Bangor and Cardiff: Cambrian Archaeological Association, Monograph 2.

Britnell, W. J. 1994. Excavation and recording at Pennant Melangell church, *Montgomeryshire Collections* 82, 41-102.

Browne, D. M. 1992. The Uplands Initiative: A Strategy for Archaeology in the Uplands of Wales, *CBA Wales-Cymru Newsletter* 3, 1-4.

Browne, D. M. 1993a. Upland Project takes off, *British Archaeological News* May 1993, 1.

Browne, D. M. 1993b. Royal Commission on Ancient and Historical Monuments in Wales. Archaeology Branch - Uplands Initiative, *Archaeology in Britain 1992*, York: Council for British Archaeology, 29-30.

Burnham, H. 1995. *A guide to ancient and historic Wales. Clwyd and Powys*, London: HMSO.

Cadw: Welsh Historic Monuments /ICOMOS 1998. *Register of Historic Parks, Gardens and Landscapes of Historic Importance in Wales. Part 2.1 Landscapes of Outstanding Historic Interest in Wales,* Cardiff: Cadw: Welsh Historic Monuments/ICOMOS.

Cadw: Welsh Historic Monuments/ ICOMOS 2001. *Register of Historic Parks, Gardens and Landscapes of Historic Importance in Wales. Part 2.2 Landscapes of Special Historic Interest in Wales,* Cardiff: Cadw: Welsh Historic Monuments/ICOMOS.

Cadw: Welsh Historic Monuments 2002. *Caring for lost farmsteads*, Cardiff: Cadw: Welsh Historic Monuments.

Campbell, S. and Bowen, D. Q. 1989. *Geological Conservation Review: Quaternary of Wales*, Peterborough: Nature Conservancy Council.

Carver, J. J., Dutton, L. A. and Muckle, P. T. 1994. *Cefn Cyfarwydd, Trefriw, upland survey 1993-1994*, Bangor: Gwynedd Archaeological Trust unpublished report.

Caseldine, A. 1990. *Environmental Archaeology in Wales*, Lampeter: Cadw and St David's University College, Lampeter.

Caseldine, A. 2003. Environmental archaeology in Wales: problems and priorities, in Briggs, C.S. (ed*) Towards a research Agenda for Welsh Archaeology*, Oxford, Archaeopress.

Cauuet, B., Ancel, B. and Cowburn, I. 2000. *The Dolaucothi Gold Mines - An Archaeological Appraisal, Intermediate Report*, Llandudno: The National Trust.

Census 1841. *Township of Upper Llanfihangel y Creuddyn, Ceredigion*, Kew: Public Record Office.

Census 1851. *Township of Upper Llanfihangel y Creuddyn, Ceredigion*, Kew: Public Record Office.

Census 1861. *Township of Upper Llanfihangel y Creuddyn, Ceredigion*, Kew: Public Record Office.

Census 1871. *Township of Upper Llanfihangel y Creuddyn, Ceredigion*, Kew: Public Record Office.

Census 1881. *Township of Upper Llanfihangel y Creuddyn, Ceredigion*, Kew: Public Record Office.

Census 1891. *Township of Upper Llanfihangel y Creuddyn, Ceredigion*, Kew: Public Record Office.

Chambers, F. M. 1982a. Environmental history of Cefn Gwernffrwd, near Rhandir mwyn mid-Wales, *New Phytologist* 92, 607-15.

Chambers, F. M. 1982b. Two radiocarbon-dated pollen diagrams from high-altitude blanket peats in south Wales, *Journal of Ecology* 70, 475-87.

Chambers, F. M. 1983a. The palaeo-ecological setting of Cefn Gwernffrwd - a prehistoric complex in mid-Wales, *Proceedings of the Prehistoric Society* 49, 303-16.

Chambers, F. M. 1983b. Three radiocarbon-dated pollen diagrams from upland peats north-west of Merthyr Tydfil, south Wales, *Journal of Ecology* 71, 475-87.

Chandler, R. H. 1909. On Some Unrecorded Boulders in South Pembroke-shire, *Geological Magazine* 6, 220-22.

Church, R. 1990. *Sennybridge Training Area 1940-90*, Cardiff: Ronald Church.

Colyer, R. 1984. *Roads and Trackways of Wales*, Ashbourne, Derbys.: Moorland Publishing.

Confederation of British Industry 1991. *Archaeological Investigations Code of Practice for Mineral Operators*, London: Confederation of British Industry.

Countryside Council for Wales 1998. *Tir Gofal: a new agri-environment scheme for Wales*, Bangor: Countryside Council for Wales.

Countryside Council for Wales and Forestry Commission 1999. A *living environment for Wales*, Bangor: Countryside Council for Wales and Forestry Commission.

Courtney, P. 1991. A native-Welsh mediaeval settlement: excavations at Beili Bedw, St Harmon, Powys, *Bulletin of the Board of Celtic Studies* 38, 233-55.

Crew, P. 1998. Excavations at Crawcwellt West, Merioneth 1990-1998, *Archaeology in Wales* 38, 22-35.

Crew, P. and Musson, C. 1996. *Snowdonia from the Air*, Penrhyndeudraeth: Snowdonia National Park Authority and RCAHMW.

Crutchley, S. 2002. Understanding Salisbury Plain, England: analysis of the aerial evidence, in Bewley, R. H. and Raczkowski, W. (eds) *Aerial Archaeology, Developing Future Practice*, Brussels: IOS Press, NATO Science Series 1: Life and Behavioural Sciences 337, 247-55.

Dark, P. 2000. *The Environment of Britain in the First Millennium A.D.*, London: Duckworth.

Darvill, T. C. 1986a. *The archaeology of the uplands: a rapid assessment of archaeological practice and knowledge*, London: RCHME and Council for British Archaeology.

Darvill, T. C. 1987a. *Upland archaeology: what future for the past?*, London: Council for British Archaeology.

Darvill, T. C. 1987b. *Ancient Monuments in the Countryside. An archaeological management review*, London: Historic Buildings and Monuments Commission for England.

Darvill, T. C. and Thomas, J. (eds) 1996. *Neolithic Houses in North west Europe and beyond*, Oxford: Oxbow Monograph 67.

Darvill, T. C. and Fulton, A. 1998. *MARS: The Monuments at Risk Survey of England, 1995. Main Report*, Bournemouth: Bournemouth University.

Davies, E. 1929. *Prehistoric and Roman remains of Denbighshire*, Cardiff: William Lewis.

Davies, E. 1949. *Prehistoric and Roman remains of Flintshire*, Cardiff: William Lewis.

Davies, J. 1974. The End of the Great Estates and the Rise of Freehold Farming in Wales, *Welsh History Review* 7, 186-212.

Davies, J. L. 1986. Careg y Bwci: a Roman watch-tower?, *Archaeologia Cambrensis* 135, 147-53.

Davies, J. L. and Lynch, F. M. 2000. The Late Bronze Age and Iron Age, in Lynch, Aldhouse-Green and Davies (eds) 2000, 139-219.

Davies, R. R. 1978. *Lordship and society in the March of Wales 1282-1400*, Oxford: Clarendon Press.

Davies, R. R. 1984. *Epynt Without People...and Much More*, Talybont, Cards.: Y Lolfa.

Davies, R. R. 1987. *Conquest, coexistence and change. Wales 1063-1415*, Oxford: Oxford University Press.

Davies, W. 1982. *Wales in the early middle ages*. Leicester: Leicester University Press.

DCC 1998. *Clwydian Range AONB upland survey. Phase 4*, Ruthin: Denbighshire County Council unpublished report.

Defence Estates 2001. *Integrated Land Management Plan, Executive Summary, Sennybridge Training Area*, Brecon: Defence Estates.

Dorling, P. J. 1994. *Summary report of BBNP upland survey 1993/4*, Brecon: Brecon Beacons National Park Authority unpublished report.

Drewett, P. L. 1987. An Archaeological Survey of Mynydd Preseli, Dyfed, *Archaeology in Wales* 27, 14-17.

Drinkwater, C. H. 1888. Ancient British hut dwellings near Bala, Merioneth, *Archaeologia Cambrensis* 5th ser., V, 26-8.

Driver, T. G. 1996. Air Photo Mapping and Record Creation Programme: Results 1995-6, *Archaeology in Wales* 36, 49-50.

Driver, T. G. 1997. *Mynydd Epynt (Sennybridge Training Area) Powys*, Aberystwyth: RCAHMW - AP Mapping Report No 1, RCAHMW unpublished report.

Driver, T. G. 1998. Mynydd Epynt (Sennybridge Training Area): RCAHM(W) Air Photo Mapping and Record Creation, Brecknockshire and Carmarthenshire, *Archaeology in Wales* 37, 27-31.

Dunning, G. C. 1943. A stone circle and cairn on Mynydd Epynt, Brecknockshire, *Archaeologia Cambrensis* 97, 169-94.

Dyer, C. C. 1989. 'The retreat from marginal land': the growth and decline of medieval rural settlements, in Aston, M., Austin, D. and Dyer, C. (eds) *The rural settlements of medieval England*, Oxford: Basil Blackwell, 45-57.

Dyer, C. C, 1995. Sheepcotes: evidence for medieval sheepfarming, *Medieval Archaeology* 39, 136-64.

Edwards, N. 2001. Early Medieval inscribed stones and stone sculpture: context and function, *Medieval Archaeology* 45, 15-39.

Evans, J. 1804. *Letters written during a tour through South Wales in the year 1803 and at other times*, London: C. and R. Baldwin.

Fasham, P. J., Kelly, R. S., Mason, M. A. and White, R. B. 1998.*The Graeanog Ridge: The Evolution of a Farming Landscape and its Settlements in North-West Wales*, Bangor: Cambrian Archaeol-ogical Association, Monograph 6.

Fleming, A. 1989. *The Dartmoor Reaves: Investigating Prehistoric Land Divisions*, London: Batsford.

Fox, A. 1939. Early Welsh homesteads on Gelligaer Common, *Archaeologia Cambrensis* 94: 163-99.

Fox, C. 1932. *The Personality of Britain*, Cardiff: National Museum and University of Wales.

Frost, P. and Scott Jones, R. 2000. *West Merthyr Tydfil Upland Survey*, Kerry, Powys: Cambrian Archaeological Projects unpublished report for RCAHMW.

Gale, F. 1995. *Clwydian Range AONB upland survey, phase 2*, Mold: Clwyd Archaeology Service unpublished report.

Gant, R. 1985. Oral history and settlement change: a case study of abandoned dwellings in the Black Mountains of Wales, 1840-1983, *Cambria* 12, 97-112.

GAT 1996. *Gwynedd upland survey 1995-96, Cadair Idris SSSI (part)*, Bangor: Gwynedd Archaeological Trust unpublished report.

Geary, K. 1998. *Bwlch Mawr-Gyrn Goch upland survey*, Bangor: Gwynedd Archaeological Trust unpublished report 288.

Gibson, A. M. 1993. Excavation of two cairns and associated features at Carneddau, Carno, Powys, *Archaeological Journal* 150, 1-45.

Glamorgan-Gwent Archaeological Trust 1997g. *Uplands Survey: Mynydd Maen and Mynydd Henllys (ST 29), Gwent*, Swansea: Glamorgan-Gwent Archaeological Trust unpublished report for RCAHMW.

Grant J. and Richardson, C. 1989. *Gwynedd inventory of ancient woodlands*, Peterborough: Nature Conservancy Council unpublished report.

Green, H. S. (ed) 1984. *Excavations at Pontnewydd Cave*, Cardiff: National Museum of Wales.

Green, S. and Walker, E. 1991. *Ice Age Hunters: Neanderthals and Early Modern Hunters in Wales*, Cardiff: National Museum of Wales.

Gresham, C. A. 1954. Platform houses in north-west Wales, *Archaeologia Cambrensis* 103, 18-53.

Gresham, C. A., Hemp, W. J. and Thompson, F. H. 1959. Hen Ddinbych, *Archaeologia Cambrensis* 108, 72-80.

Griffith, M. 1989. Manganese Mining at Rhiw in Llyn between 1827 and 1945, *Transactions of the Caernarvonshire Historical Society* 50, 41-70.

Gwyn, D. R. 2000. *Caring for the Industrial Heritage of Slate*, Bangor: Gwynedd Archaeological Trust.

Gwynedd Archaeological Trust 1998. *Moel Bowydd Upland Survey, GAT Report no. 199*, Bangor: Gwynedd Archaeological Trust unpublished report for RCAHMW.

Hampton, J. N., Palmer, R. & Clark, A. J. 1977. Implications of Aerial Photography for Archaeology, *Archaeol Jnl.*, 134, 157-95.

Hankinson, R. 1995b *Pentrefoelas windfarm, Clwyd*, Welshpool: Clwyd-Powys Archaeological Trust unpublished report.

Hankinson, R., Jones, N. W., Dorling, P. and Thomas, D. R. 1998. *Black Mountains upland survey*, Welshpool: Clwyd-Powys Archaeological Trust unpublished report.

Hankinson, R. and Thomas, D. 1999. *The North Radnorshire Commons Survey*, Welshpool: Clwyd-Powys Archaeological Trust unpublished report for RCAHMW.

Harris, A. and Spratt, D. 1991. The rabbit warrens of the Tabular Hills, north Yorkshire, *Yorkshire Archaeological Journal* 63, 177-206.

Hayman, R. and Horton, W. 2000. *Blaenafon North-west Upland Survey*, Shrewsbury: a Hayman and Horton unpublished report for RCAHMW.

Hayman. R. and Horton. W. 2001. *Blaenafon East Upland Survey*, Shrewsbury: a Hayman and Horton unpublished report for RCAHMW.

Hearne, T. 1745. *The Itinerary of John Leland The Antiquary*, second edition vol. 5, pp.77-83. From the original MS in the Bodleian Library. Published at The Theatre, Oxford.

Hopewell, D. 2000. *Gwynedd upland survey 1999-2000, Moel Bowydd, Blaenau Ffestiniog*, Bangor: Gwynedd Archaeological Trust unpublished report.

Hooke, D. 1997. Place-names and vegetation history as a key to understanding settlement in the Conwy Valley, in Edwards, N. (ed) *Landscape and settlement in medieval Wales*, Oxford: Oxbow Monograph 81, 78-95.

http://www.bbc.co.uk/history/genes/population/population_dna.shtml

Hudson, K. 1984. *Industrial history from the air*, Cambridge: Cambridge University Press.

Hughes, H. 1997. '*Mae'n Ddiwedd Byd Yma...', Mynydd Epynt a'r Troad Allan yn 1940*, Llandysul: Gomer.

Hughes, S. J. 1981. The Cwmystwyth Mines, *British Mining* 17, Sheffield: Northern Mine Research Society.

Hughes, S. R. 1990. *The Archaeology of an Early Railway System: The Brecon Forest Tramroads*, Aberystwyth: RCAHMW.

Hughes, S. R. 1994. Hushing Channels at Cwmystwyth, in Ford, T. and Willies, L. (eds) Mining Before Powder, *Bulletin Peak District Mines Historical Society* 12: 3, 37-40.

Hughes, S. R. 2000. *Copperopolis: Early Industrial Landscapes at Swansea*, Aberystwyth: RCAHMW.

ICOMOS 2000. ICOMOS Report to the World Heritage Committee 2000.

James, H. J. 1994. The archaeology of the early church in Cardiganshire, in Davies, J. L. and Kirby, D. J. (eds), *The County History of Cardiganshire, Vol.1*, Cardiff: University of Wales Press, 397-407.

Jenkins, D. A. and Timberlake, S. 1997. *Geoarchaeological Research into Prehistoric Mining for Copper in Wales*, Bangor: University of Wales Bangor unpublished report to the Leverhulme Trust.

Johnson, N. and Rose, P. 1994. *Bodmin Moor. An archaeological survey. Volume 1: the human landscape to c 1800*, London: English Heritage.

Jones, G. D. B., Blakey, I. J. and Macpherson, E. C. F. 1960. Dolaucothi: The Roman Aqueduct, *Bulletin of the Board of Celtic Studies* 19, 71-84.

Jones, S. G. 1995. *Gwynedd upland survey: Moel Bronymiod*, Bangor: Gwynedd Archaeological Trust unpublished report.

Kelly, R. S. 1982. The Ardudwy Survey: fieldwork in western Merioneth, 1971-81, *Journal of the Merioneth Historical Record Society* 9:2, 121-62.

Kelly, R. S. 1983. A pre-afforestation survey of Cy Fannedd, Arthog, Gwynedd, *Bulletin of the Board of Celtic Studies* 30, 441-52.

Kelly, R. S. 1990. Recent research on the hut group settlements of north-west Wales, in Burnham, B. C. and Davies, J. L. (eds) *Conquest, co-existence and change*, Lampeter: St David's University College, *Trivium*, 25, 102-111.

Kerkham, C. R. 1991. Hafod: Paradise Lost, *Journal of Garden History* 11, 207-16.

Kerkham, C. R. and Briggs, C. S. 1991. The Archaeological Potential of the Hafod Demesne, in Brown, A. E. (ed) *Garden Archaeology*, London: Council for British Archaeology, Research Report 78.

Khan, M. 1995. Sennybridge Training Area, *After The Battle* 90, 42-9.

King, D. J. C. 1961. The Castles of Breconshire, *Brycheiniog* 7, 71-94.

Knight, J. K. 1978. Early Christian origins and society in South Wales, *Merthyr Historian* 2, 101-110.

Knight, J. K. 1989. *Blaenafon Ironworks*, Cardiff: Cadw.

Lamb, H. H. 1981. Climate from 1000 BC to 1000 AD, in Jones, M. and Dimbleby, G. (eds) *The environment of man*, Oxford: British Archaeological Reports 87, 53-65.

Laun, J. van 1979. Hill Pits, Blaenafon, *Industrial Archaeology Review* 3: 3, 258-75.

Lawler, M., Walker, M. J. C. and Locock, M. 1997. A cairnfield at Cefn-yr-Esgyrn, mid-Glamorgan: an archaeological and palaeoenvironmental study, *Studia Celtica* 31, 83-105.

Leighton, D. K. 1997. *Mynydd Du and Fforest Fawr: the evolution of an upland landscape in South Wales*, Aberystwyth: RCAHMW.

Lewin, R. 1997. Ancestral echoes, *New Scientist* 2089, 32-7.

Lewis, C. A. 1996. *Prehistoric mining at the Great Orme: criteria for the identification of early mining*, Bangor: University of Wales Bangor unpublished M. Phil. Thesis.

Lewis, S. 1833. *A Topographical Dictionary of Wales*, London: S.Lewis.

Lewis, W. J. 1967. *Lead Mining in Wales*, Cardiff: University of Wales Press.

Linnard, W. 1982. *Welsh Woods and Forests: History and Utilization*, Llandysal: Gomer, 2000, 108-20.

Locock, M. 1997. *Uplands survey: Mynydd Maen and Mynydd Henllys (ST 29), Gwent*, Swansea: Glamorgan-Gwent Archaeological Trust unpublished report.

Locock, M. 2000. *Deserted rural settlements in Glamorgan*, Swansea: Glamorgan-Gwent Archaeological Trust unpublished report.

Lowe, J. and Lawlor, M. 1980. Landscapes of the Iron Industry at Blaenafon, Gwent, *Landscape History* 2, 74-82.

Lowe, J. 1985. *Welsh Industrial Workers Housing 1775-85*, 2nd edition, Cardiff: National Museum of Wales.

Lynch, F. M. 1972. Ring-cairns and related monuments in Wales, *Scottish Archaeological Forum* 4, 61-80.

Lynch, F. M. 1979. Ring cairns in Britain and Ireland: their design and purpose, *Ulster Journal of Archaeology* 42, 1-19.

Lynch, F. M. 1986. Excavation of a Kerb Circle and Ring Cairn on Cefn Caer Euni, Merioneth, *Archaeologia Cambrensis* 135, 81-120.

Lynch, F. M. 1993. *Excavations in the Brenig Valley: a Mesolithic and Bronze Age Landscape in North Wales,* Cardiff: Cambrian Archaeological. Association, Monograph 5.

Lynch, F. M. 2000.The Earlier Neolithic; The Later Neolithic and Bronze Age, in Lynch, Aldhouse-Green and Davies 2000, 42-78.

Lynch, F. M., Aldhouse-Green, S. H. R. and Davies, J. L. 2000. *Prehistoric Wales*, Stroud: Sutton Publishing.

Manley, J. 1986. Fields, farms and funerary monuments on Mynydd Poeth, Clwyd, *Bulletin of the Board of Celtic Studies* 33, 387-413.

Manley, J. 1990. A Late Bronze Age landscape on the Denbigh Moors, northeast Wales, *Antiquity* 64, 514-26.

Marshall, E. C. and Murphy, K. 1991. The excavation of two Bronze Age cairns with associated standing stones in Dyfed: Parc Maen and Abercamddwr II, *Archaeologia Cambrensis* 140, 28-76.

Mighall, T. M. and Chambers, F. M. 1993. The environmental impact of prehistoric copper mining at Copa Hill, Cwmystwyth, Wales, *The Holocene* 3, 260-4.

Moore-Colyer, R. 2001. *Roads and trackways of Wales*, Ashbourne: Landmark Publishing.

Moore, D. 1976. Cambrian antiquity: precursors of the prehistorians, in Boon, G. C. and Lewis, J. M. (eds) *Welsh Antiquity*, Cardiff: National Museum of Wales, 193-211.

Moore, D. 1997. Thomas Pennant's view of the landscape, *Archaeologia Cambrensis* 146, 138-77.

Morgan, G. 1991. Early Hafod tenants and the founding of the estate, *Friends of Hafod Newsletter* 9, 5-7.

Morgan, J. G. and Ruggles, C. L. N. 1976. Indications at the Cefn Gwernffrwd site, *Archaeologia Cambrensis* 125, 162-5.

Muckle, P. T. 1996. *Moel Llechwedd-gwyn, upland survey 1995/96*, private unpublished survey.

Murphy, K. nd. *Hafod Database*, Llandeilo: unpublished data held at Cambria Archaeology.

Murphy, K. 1999. *Upland Ceredigion:Historic Landscape Characterisation,* Llandeilo:Cambria Archaeology unpublished report.

Musson, C. R. 1993. *Shropshire from the Air*, Shrewsbury: Shropshire County Council.

Musson, C. R. 1994. *Wales from the Air: Patterns of Past and Present*, Aberystwyth: RCAHMW.

Musson, C. R., Britnell, W. J. and Smith, A.G. 1991. *The Breidden Hillfort: A Later Prehistoric Settlement in the Welsh Marches*, London: Council for British Archaeology, Research Report 76.

National Assembly for Wales, 2001. *Woodlands for Wales. The National Assembly for Wales Strategy for Trees and Woodlands*, Aberystwyth: Forestry Commission.

Newman, R. 2001. *The historical archaeology of Britain, c.1540-1900*, Stroud: Sutton Publishing.

Owen, T. M. 1975. Historical aspects of peat-cutting in Merioneth, *Journal of the Merioneth Record Society* 7: 3, 308-21.

Owen, T. M. 1990. *Torri mawn*, Llanrwst: Gwasg Carreg Gwalch.

Parry, M. L. 1985. Upland settlement and climatic change, in Spratt, D. and Burgess, C. (eds) *Upland Settlement in Britain. The second millennium BC and after*, Oxford: British Archaeological Reports, British Series 143, 35-49.

Parry, T. B. 1964. The Blorenge: a study of old ironworkings on the Blorenge mountain in Monmouthshire, *Journal of Industrial Archaeology* 1, 77-93.

Percival, D. J. 1996. *East Merthyr Survey Archive*, Aberystwyth: National Monuments Record of Wales unpublished report.

Pilcher, J. R. and Hall, V. A. 1996. A Tephrochronology for the Holocene of the north of Ireland, *The Holocene* 2, 255-9.

Powell, T. G. E. 1973. Excavation of the Megalithic Chambered Cairn at Dyffryn Ardudwy, Merioneth, Wales, *Archaeologia* 104, 1-49.

Protheroe-Jones, R. 1993. *Ceredigion Metal Mines Survey*, Llandeilo: Dyfed Archaeological Trust unpublished report for RCAHMW.

RCAHMW 1937. *An Inventory of the Ancient Monuments in Anglesey*, London: HMSO.

RCAHMW 1956, *An Inventory of the Ancient Monuments in Caernarvonshire. Vol I: East*, London: HMSO.

RCAHMW 1960. *An Inventory of the Ancient Monuments in Caernarvonshire. Vol II: Central*, London: HMSO.

RCAHMW 1964. *An Inventory of the Ancient Monuments in Caernarvonshire. Vol III: West*, London: HMSO.

RCAHMW 1976. *An Inventory of the Ancient Monuments in Glamorgan. Vol I (part III): The Early Christian Period*, Cardiff: HMSO.

RCAHMW 1982. *An Inventory of the Ancient Monuments in Glamorgan. Volume III: Medieval Secular Monuments, Part II, Non-defensive*, Cardiff: HMSO.

RCAHMW 1986. *An Inventory o/ the Ancient Monuments in Brecknock (Brycheiniog): The Prehistoric and Roman Monuments; Part ii: Hill-forts and Roman remains*, London: HMSO.

RCAHMW 1997. *An Inventory of the Ancient Monuments in Brecknock (Brycheiniog), The Prehistoric and Roman Monuments; Part i: Later Prehistoric Monuments and Unenclosed Settlements to 1000AD*, Aberystwyth: RCAHMW.

Rees, I. B. (ed) 1992. *The mountains of Wales*, Cardiff: University of Wales Press.

Sambrook, P. 1999. *The Mynydd y Ffynnon Project Phase V: site management report*, Llandeilo: Cambria Archaeology unpublished report.

Sambrook, P. 2000. *An upland glossary for Wales*, Llandeilo: Dyfed Archaeological Trust unpublished report for RCAHMW.

Sambrook, P. 2001. *The Mynydd y Ffynnon Project Phase VI (2000-1 Survey)*, Llandeilo: Cambria Archaeology unpublished report.

Sambrook, P. and Darke, I. 1997. *The Mynydd y Ffynnon Project-Castell Rheidol upland survey*, Llandeilo: Dyfed Archaeological Trust unpublished survey.

Sambrook, P. and Ramsey, R. 1998. *Deserted rural settlement study 1997-8*, Llandeilo: Cambria Archaeology unpublished report.

Sambrook, P., Benson, D., Hall, J. and Wilson, H. 1999. *Review of Upland Archaeology in Dyfed: 1989-99*, Llandeilo: Dyfed Archaeological Trust unpublished report for RCAHMW.

Silvester, R. J. 1990. The Carno/Dwyrhiw (Montgomeryshire) survey, *Archaeology in Wales* 30, 35-6.

Silvester, R. J. 1992. *The Radnor Forest upland survey*, Welshpool: Clwyd-Powys Archaeological Trust unpublished report 33.

Silvester, R. J. 1994. Lake Vyrnwy Area (SJ 01932301), *Archaeology in Wales* 34, 50-1.

Silvester, R. J. 1995. Pillow mounds at Y Foel, Llanllugan, *Montgomeryshire Collections* 83, 75-90.

Silvester, R. J. 1996. *Pennant, Llandrillo, Denbighshire*, Welshpool: Clwyd-Powys Archaeological Trust unpublished report 173.

Silvester, R. J. 1997a. *The Mynydd y Ffynnon Landscape Survey II*, Welshpool: Clwyd-Powys Archaeological Trust unpublished report 234.

Silvester, R. J. 1997b. Welsh antiquarian societies and field clubs in the nineteenth century, *Monmouthshire Antiquary* 13, 30-6.

Silvester, R J. 1997c. The Llanwddyn Hospitium, *Montgomeryshire Collections* 85, 63-76.

Silvester, R. J. 1999. *Uplands Fieldwork in Clwyd and Powys 1989-1999: a synthesis*, Welshpool: Clwyd-Powys Archaeological Trust unpublished report 318.

Silvester, R. J. 2000. Medieval upland cultivation on the Berwyns in north Wales, *Landscape History* 22, 47-60.

Silvester, R. J. forthcoming a. Deserted settlements in central and north-east Wales, in *Deserted Rural settlements in Wales*, Cardiff: Cadw.

Silvester, R. J. forthcoming b. The commons and waste: use and misuse in central Wales, *Landscape History*.

Silvester, R. J. and Hankinson, R. 1995. *Ruabon Mountain Uplands Survey*, Welshpool: Clwyd-Powys Archaeological Trust unpublished report for RCAHMW.

Simmons, I. G. 1996. *The Environmental Impact of Later Mesolithic Cultures*, Edinburgh: Edinburgh University Press.

Skeates, R. 1997. The Brecon Beacons archaeological survey, *Archaeology in Wales* 37, 32-46.

Smith, A. G. and Cloutman, E. W. 1988. Reconstruction of Holocene vegetation history in three dimensions at Waun-Fignen-Felen, an upland site in South Wales, *Philosophical Transactions of the Royal Society London* B322, 159-219.

Smith, C. A. and Lynch, F. M. 1987. *Trefignath and Din Dryfol: the Excavation of two Megalithic Tombs in Anglesey*, Cardiff: Cambrian Archaeological Association, Monograph 3.

Smith, G. 1999. Survey of prehistoric and Romano-British settlement in north-west Wales, *Archaeologia Cambrensis* 148, 22-53.

Smith, K. E. S. 1995. Iron-working in north-west Wales in the late fourteenth century, *Archaeological Journal* 152, 246-90.

Sykes, B. 1999a. *The Human Inheritance: Genes Language and Evolution*, Oxford: Oxford University Press.

Sykes, B. 1999b. The Molecular genetics of European ancestry, *Proceedings of the Royal Society* 354, 131-39.

Taylor, J. A. 1980. *Culture and Environment in Prehistoric Wales*, Oxford: British Archaeological Reports.

Thom, A. S. 1967. *Megalithic Lunar Observatories*, Oxford: Oxford University Press.

Thomas, H. J. 1984. Iolo Morganwg vindicated: Glamorgan's first field archaeologist, *Glamorgan Gwent Archaeological Trust Report*, 149-57.

Thomas, W.G. 1981. *Big Pit, Blaenafon*, Cardiff: National Museum of Wales.

Thompson, D. 1997. *Deserted rural settlement in western Caernarfonshire*, Bangor: Gwynedd Archaeological Trust unpublished report.

Thompson, D. 1998a. *Deserted rural settlement in eastern Caernarfonshire*, Bangor: Gwynedd Archaeological Trust unpublished report.

Thompson, D. 1998b. *Moel Bowydd Archaeological Survey*, Bangor: Gwynedd Archaeological Trust unpublished report.

Thompson, D. 2000. *Mapping Historical Tide-marks: Upland Survey in Gwynedd (1983-2000)*, Bangor: Gwynedd Archaeological Trust unpublished report.

Thompson, D. and Yates, M. 1999. Deserted rural settlement in Wales – a framework for study, a strategy for protection, in Fridrich, J. (ed) *Ruralia III*, Prague: Institute of Archaeology.

Thompson, M. W. 1983. *The journeys of Sir Richard Colt Hoare through Wales and England, 1793-1810*, Gloucester: Allan Sutton.

Timberlake, S. 1988. Excavations at Parys Mountain and Nantyreira, *Archaeology in Wales* 28, 50.

Timberlake, S. 1990. Excavation and fieldwork on Copa Hill, Cwmystwyth, in Crew, P. and Crew, S. (eds) *Early Mining in the British Isles*, Maentwrog: Snowdonia Study Centre, Occasional Paper 1.

Timberlake, S. 1992. Llancynfelin and Nantyrarian Mines, *Archaeology in Wales* 32, 90-1.

Timberlake, S. and Mighall, T. 1992. Historic and prehistoric mining on Copa Hill, Cwmystwyth, *Archaeology in Wales* 32: 38-44.

Timberlake, S. 1994. Archaeological and circumstantial evidence for early mining in Wales, *Bulletin of the Peak District Mines Historical Society*.12: 3, 133-43.

Timberlake, S. 1995. Copa Hill and Llancynfelin Mine, *Archaeology in Wales* 35, 40-3.

Timberlake, S. 1996. Ogof Copper Mine, Llanymynech; Tyn y Fron Mine; Pen Cerrig y Mwyn, *Archaeology in Wales* 36, 68-70; 61-3; 104-105.

Timberlake, S. 2001. Early Metal Mining Research in the UK: the developments of the last 10 years, in Craddock, P. T. and Lang, J. (eds) *Aspects of Early Mining and Metallurgy*, London: British Museum Press

Timberlake, S. 2002. forthcoming paper in Claughton, P. (ed) *Waterpower Leats in Mining* quoting radiocarbon dates from peat in silted leats (B-analytic Laboratory).

Timeteam Excavation at Blaenafon, Channel 4, 4 February 2001: http://www.channel4.com/history/timeteam/archive/2001ba.html

UNESCO 1999. *The Operational Guidelines for the Implementation of the World Heritage Convention*, Paris: UNESCO, 9.

Walker, E. 2003. Moving the Palaeolithic and Mesolithic of Wales into the Future, in Briggs, C. S. (ed) 2003, 79-89.

Ward, A. H. 1988. Aspects of the siting of cairns in south-west Wales with particular reference to ring cairns, *Bulletin of the Board of Celtic Studies* 35, 92-105.

Ward, A H. 1989. Land allotment of possible prehistoric date on Mynydd Llangyndeyrn, south-east Dyfed, *Archaeologia Cambrensis* 138, 46-58.

Ward, J. 1915. St Nicholas Chambered Tumulus, Glamorgan, *Archaeologia Cambrensis* 69, 253-320.

Ward, J. 1916. St Nicholas Chambered Tumulus, Glamorgan, *Archaeologia Cambrensis* 70, 239-67.

WAT nd. *Archaeology in the Welsh Uplands: an Initial Assessment*, Abergwili: Welsh Archaeological Trusts unpublished report to Cadw: Welsh Historic Monuments.

Welsh Office. *Welsh Office Circular 60/96 Planning and the Historic Environment: Archaeology*, Cardiff: Welsh Office.

Welsh Assembly Government 2002. *Planning Policy Wales*, Cardiff: Welsh Assembly Government.

Whimster, R. 1981. *Burial Practices in Iron Age Britain*, Oxford: British Archaeological Reports, British Series 90.

Whimster, R. 1989. *The Emerging Past*, London: HMSO.

Wickham-Jones, C. R. 2001. *The landscape of Scotland*, Stroud: Tempus.

Wiliam, E. 1986. *The historical farm buildings of Wales*, Edinburgh: John Donald.

Williams, D. H. 1965. Cistercians in Wales: some aspects of their economy, *Archaeologia Cambrensis* 114, 2-47.

Williams, D. H. 1990. *An atlas of the Cistercians in Wales*, Cardiff: University of Wales Press.

Williams, D. H. 2001. *The Welsh Cistercians*, Leominster: Gracewing.

Williams, G. H. 1985. A group of burnt mounds at Morfa Mawr, Aberaeron, *Ceredigion* 10, 181-8.

Williams, G .H. 1988. *The Standing Stones of Wales and South West England*, Oxford: British Archaeological Reports, British Series 197.

Williams, G. and Darke, I. 1996. *Mynydd Mallaen survey 1995*, Abergwili: Dyfed Archaeological Trust unpublished report.

Williams, G. and Muckle, P. 1992. *An archaeological survey of the Groes Fawr valley, Caron-is-clawdd, Cardiganshire*, Llandeilo: Cambria Archaeology unpublished report.

Winchester, A. J. L. 2000. *The harvest of the hills*, Edinburgh: Edinburgh University Press.

Wymer, J. J. 1999. *The Lower Palaeolithic Occupation of Britain*, Salisbury: The Trust for Wessex Archaeology and English Heritage.

www.bbc.co.uk/history

Yates, A. M. 1998. *Uplands survey: Mynydd y Garth, Mynydd Uchaf and Cefn Gwrhyd, Neath and Port Talbot (SN 70 and SN 71)*, Swansea: Glamorgan-Gwent Archaeological Trust unpublished report.

INDEX

Page numbers in italic refer to illustration captions.

South Wales Coalfield, 61, *65*
spoil tips/heaps, 46, *55*, *63*, 73, *99*, *115*, 133, *133*, *see also* waste tips
squatters' settlements: Bryngwyn Bach (Ceredigion), *56*; Cwmystwyth (Ceredigion), 56; iron-workers (Merthyr Tydfil), *59*
St Joseph, Dr J. K. S., 12-13
St Peter's School complex (Blaenafon), 106, 124
standing stones, 25, 125; Maen Llia, *24*, 28; Maen Mawr, *12*; Moel Bronymiod Survey Area, 78; platform cairn Brenig 51, *13*; Ysbyty Cynfyn church, 70
Stapledon, Sir George, 100-1
stells, 130
stock enclosures, 78, 127
stone axes, 22
stone circles, *12*, 25, 88, 125, *125*
stone rows, 25, *27*
stone settings, 125
Stonehenge (Wilts), 9
Strata Florida Abbey (Ceredigion), 34; land in possession of, *70*, 71-2, *71*, *72*; rent rolls, 71, 72
Strata Marcella (Powys), 34
stratigraphy, 124
subsidence: drift mines and, 67
summer dairies, 37
'sunken shelter': Cwmystwyth, 72
sunken stores, 129
SUSTRANS national cycle trail, 106

Tafarn-y-Mynydd (Epynt), 91
Taff valley (Glam): inscribed stones, 32
Tai Newyddion (Cwmystwyth), 56, *58*, 74
tai unnos, 37, 56, *56*, 129
Tal-y-garreg (Gwynedd), *111*
Tanat valley (Montgomeryshire), 32
Tarenig valley (Montgomeryshire), 69, 70
Tawe, river, *12*
Tir Gofal, 109, 113, 114, 118
Tir-cyd (Epynt): house footings, 95-6, 97, *97*
tombs: Megalithic, 22-3, *22*, *23*
Tomen y Mur, *14*, *15*, 28
Torfaen Borough Council, 107, 124
Torfaen Museum Trust, 13
tourism, 109; Big Pit mining museum, *48*, *53*, 64, 67, 105, 106; Brecknock and Abergavenny Canal, 105, 106, *107*; cause of erosion, *113*, 118, *121*; Disgwylfa visitor centre (Epynt), 97, *101*; Pontypool and Blaenafon Railway Company, 105-6; Pwllpeiran Agritourism project, 102-3, *see also* Blaenafon World Heritage Project; recreational activities

trackways, 39, 131; Mynydd Cil-cwm (Llanbrynmair), *40*; Mynydd Epynt, 91, 93
tramways/tramroads, *2*, 46; Blaenafon, 62, *63*, *64*, *65*, 67, 105, *106*, *see also* railways
transhumance (stock movement), 34-5, 118, 120
Trawsfynydd (Meirionydd): Crawcwellt hut circles, *127*; Fridd Bod y Fuddau, hut group, *27*; Prince Edward gold mine, 41
Trecastell (Caerns), 44
Tredegar, 59
Tregaron, 32
Tre'r Ceiri (Caerns), 12, 27, 78
Tri Chrugiau (Epynt), 88
Trum y Wern (Berwyns), 85
tunnels: railways and tramroads, 53, *60*, 62, *63*, *65*
turnpike roads, *60*
Twll y Mwyn (Ceredigion), 44
Twrch valley (Carms), *32*, *33*
Tygwyn farmstead (Ceredigion), 72, 73
Tyla quarries (Blaenafon), 67
Tyllwyd (Cwmystwyth), *74*
Tyn y Fron (Ceredigion), 44
Ty'n yr Ochr (Ceredigion), 55

upland antiquities: study of, 10-14
Upland Glossary of Wales, 125
upland stations (*hafodydd*), 35, 71-2
Uplands: economic potential of, 99-103
Uplands Forum, 17
Uplands Initiative, *7*, 14-17, 29, 114; achievements of, 117-18; Y Berwyn, 82; Blaenafon, 61, *62*; coal mining landscapes, 48; future of, 118-24; industrial settlements, 55; site preservation and management, 109-13
Uplands Steering Committee, 17
Urban Commons, 106
Uwch Gwyrfai (Caerns), 77

Vigra gold mine (Meirionydd), 41

Wagstaff Lead Vein: (Halkyn/Helygain, Flints), 44, 45
Wales Tourist Board, 107
Ward, Anthony, 13
Warren, The (Epynt), 95, *95*
waste tips: Dowlais, *115*; Gorseddau slate quarry, *2*; ironstone (Blaenafon), 67; Nant Cwm Tywyll, 86; Penydarren workers' settlement, 59, *see also* spoil tips/heaps
water-balance lifts, 67
water engines, 46

water power, 117; Blaenafon, *65*, 117; impact of alternative energy schemes, 112
water pumping, 46
water-scouring (hushing), 45, *46*, *47*, 51, *63*, *65*, *66*, 67, 117, 120, 133
water-wheels, *2*, 46, 47
watercourses: artificial, 123, 133, *see also* leats
Waun Fignen Felen (Brecknocks), 21
Waun-fawr farm (Epynt), *90*
Welsh Archaeological Trusts, 13, 17, 109, 113, 118
Welsh Assembly Government, 106, 110
Welsh Development Agency, 107
Welsh Heritage Assets Survey, 113
Welsh Historic Assets (WHA) Survey, 114
Williams-Wynn, Watkin, 82
windfarm: Llidiart-y-waun, *108*
wind turbine power stations: impact of, 110, 112; Llidiartywaun (Powys), *108*
women: lead mine employees, 56, 57; race and language, 123
Woodland Grant Schemes, 113
World Heritage Landscapes *see* Blaenafon World Heritage Project/Site
Wye valley, 17, 69

Ynyshir (Epynt), 88
Ynyspandy (Gwynedd), *2*
Ysbyty Cynfyn church (Ceredigion), 70
Ysgir Fawr valley (Epynt), 91-3, *91*, *93*
Ysgir Fechan valley (Epynt), 91, 93-4, *94*
Ystrad Meurig (Ceredigion), 59
Ystwyth valley, 17, 69; development of modern landscape, 99-100; evidences of Bronze Age settlement, 70; medieval *hafod* settlements, 72; Pwllpeiran experimental farm, 69, 72, 99, 100-3, *101-3*, *see also* Cwmystwyth

zinc mining, 41, 57